# BUILT ON FAITH

*Transform Your Life with Affirmative Prayer*

Lezli Goodwin

Copyright © 2017, 2019 by Lezli Goodwin. All rights reserved.

All rights reserved. No part of this publication may be reproduced, distributed or transmitted in any form or by any means including photocopying, recording or other electronic or mechanical methods, or by any information storage and retrieval system without the prior written consent of the publisher, except in the case of very brief quotations and other noncommercial uses permitted by copyright law.

First Printing: March, 2019

INFINITE SPIRIT PRESS

Infinite Spirit Press
Phoenix, Arizona

# FROM THE AUTHOR

I am Lezli Goodwin, professional spiritual mentor, minister and affirmative prayer enthusiast. I believe that committed, powerful daily prayer will change the world. It is my deepest passion to help people find their own path to prayer and experience the life they desire.

For over 15 years I've been helping people connect with the God of their understanding, helping my clients and students utilize what they already know through one-on-one spiritual mentoring, affirmative prayer calls, classes, workshops and public speaking engagements. More than anything, I'm sought out for my powerful, heartfelt affirmative prayers. It is my pleasure to share the bits of wisdom I've collected with you, and it is my deepest hope that you will utilize this book to connect with the Divine and reveal more Spiritual Truth in your life.

## *The Bottom Line*

I'm a Spiritual Mentor, sure. That's my day job and my reason for being. I'm also the matriarch of a big, bustling family (five kids, two dogs, a cat, a husband, random stragglers). I'm a singer/songwriter of Posi (positive) music. I love to bead, paint, crochet -- anything artsy is my cup of tea. I love days where I hole-up in my tiny office, meditating and/or playing on Facebook with my hair in a messy bun and wearing yoga pants. I'm a real person. I mess up sometimes. But you better believe I take those mistakes straight to prayer, to feel the Power and the Presence of Spirit making things right. That's the life I want for you. Let's do this, together!

# GRATITUDE

I received a tremendous amount of help in the creation of this book, and give grateful thanks to everyone who offered their assistance and support. I tried for quite awhile to edit this list down to fit on one page, but then I decided that too much gratitude is never a bad thing. Huge thanks to Rev. Jeffrey Kealoha Ryan, Rev. Sonia Byrne, Tina Vlassie, Pam Wake and Diane Riebesehl for your careful (and much needed) proof reading. They say it takes a village, and it certainly took all five of you to put Humpty Dumpty back together again.

Thank you to the members of the *Wisdom Everyday* Facebook group for offering prayer suggestions, love and support. Our tribe is deeply precious to me, and I adore every one of you. Extra special thanks to tribe members Emily Abbas, Jen Day, Sandy Hemenway, Maureen Geraghty, Kathleen McIntosh, Mindy Stevens, Beth Weller, Karen Oschmann, Hector Quiroz Jr., Lisa Petrich, Christina Smith, Shawn Madden, Pam Wake, Derek Marmon and Jill Gibbs for prayer suggestions that made it into this book.

My heartfelt gratitude to all of the friends, teachers, mentors and ministers who have nurtured me in my spiritual pursuits. Endless love and appreciation to Rev. Kathleen Sibley, Rev. Dr. Penny Macek, Rev. Dr. Kathy Hearn, Rev. Dr. Michelle Medrano, Rev. Kevin Bucy, Rev. Kathryn McDowell, Dawn Kerlin, Brad Wentker, Beverley Strutt, Karen Blakeley, Rev. Kimjera Whittington, Rev. Nicole Von Atzingen, Rev. Sonia Byrne and Rev. Jeffrey Kealoha Ryan. Special thanks to my friend and constant cheerleader, Jennifer Mobley, who always knew I could do this.

Big thanks to my kids for putting up with a distracted, busy Mom when I'm writing. It's a source of deep inspiration to watch you become that people that you are meant to be: strong, courageous, creative, intelligent souls that will change the world. Christopher, Lauren, Melody, Creighton, Dharma – you are my "why".

Finally, none of this would be possible without the endless support of my husband. Bobby, thanks for making sure I eat, offering me hot beverages, and not getting annoyed when I yell at you to stop offering me hot beverages. You're a catch.

# TABLE OF CONTENTS

Built on Faith .................................................................................................1
From the Author ...........................................................................................1
Gratitude .......................................................................................................2
**Table of Contents** ....................................................................................4
All About Affirmative Prayer ........................................................................7
    Foundational Assumptions ...................................................................10
    How It Works .........................................................................................12
Writing Your Own Affirmative Prayers ......................................................15
    The Three Prep Steps ............................................................................16
    Step One: Recognition ..........................................................................19
    Step Two: Unification ...........................................................................21
    Step Three: Realization ........................................................................24
    Step Four: Thanksgiving .......................................................................28
    Step Five: Release .................................................................................31
Taking Things Further ................................................................................35
    Daily Prayer, Whether You Need It or Not ..........................................35
    Praying Out Loud ..................................................................................39
    Praying for Someone Else ....................................................................42
    Prayer Partner Relationships ...............................................................51
    Praying For Groups ...............................................................................55
Affirmative Prayer Library .........................................................................58
    Prayer for Health ..................................................................................60
    Prayer to Prepare for Surgery ..............................................................61
    Prayer for Faith and Surrender ............................................................63
    Prayer for Peace of Mind .....................................................................64
    Prayer for Clarity ..................................................................................65
    Prayer for Focus ...................................................................................66
    Prayer for Creativity .............................................................................67
    Prayer for Joy .......................................................................................68
    Prayer to Release Overwhelm .............................................................69
    Prayer for Acceptance and Tolerance .................................................70
    Prayer for Blessing a New Baby ...........................................................71

- Prayer for Wisdom for our World Leaders ......72
- Prayer for Financial Abundance ......74
- Prayer for the Perfect Job ......75
- Prayer for a Successful Meeting ......77
- Prayer to Sell a House ......78
- Prayer for a New Romantic Partner ......80
- Prayer for a Healed Relationship ......82
- Prayer for Forgiveness ......83
- Prayer to Release the Past ......85
- Prayer for Grief ......86
- Prayer of Gratitude ......87
- Prayer for Full Expression ......88
- Prayer for Balance ......89
- Prayer for My Highest and Best ......90

Resources ......91
- Ways to Learn More ......91
- Template for 5-Step Affirmative Prayer ......95
- List of Spiritual Qualities ......97
- List of Names for God ......98

*"When prayer removes distrust and doubt and enters the field of mental certainty, it becomes faith; and the universe is built on faith."*

Ernest Holmes

# ALL ABOUT AFFIRMATIVE PRAYER

I vividly remember my first experience with affirmative prayer. It was my first Sunday at New Vision Center for Spiritual Living in Phoenix, Arizona. I remember the words pouring over me like liquid calm and a feeling of peace descending. The prayer was unlike anything I had ever heard before, full of confidence that everything needed was already given by Divine Goodness. Something in me knew that I had found my spiritual home. I wanted that confidence, that absolute surety that God was right where I am, but I never dreamed that I could pray like that woman on the pulpit. This was before I knew about affirmative prayer or that it was a skill set that anyone can learn and use in their own life. All I knew was that I wanted to feel that feeling of safety and love and peace every day for the rest of my life.

If you were drawn to this book, I'm willing to bet that you are seeking the same thing – a deeper sense of the Divine in your own life. I've often heard it said, "The only thing wrong with your workout is that you're not doing it." I believe the same to be true about spiritual practice. We spiritual-but-not-religious-folks have a tendency to be seekers and explorers, but we're not always the best appliers of the information we find. See if any of this applies to you:

- You've read lots of books on self-improvement and manifestation, but you haven't put most of the suggested activities into regular practice.
- You've taken classes on prayer and meditation, but don't usually take time for a daily spiritual practice.
- A part of you still thinks of beautiful, flowing, spontaneous prayer as something other people do – special people with special training – so you don't really try.

Here's the truth: If you've read more than five spiritual books, there's probably not much I could throw at you that you haven't already encountered. That's not what this book is about. You don't need to learn more right now. You need to practice what you've already learned until it's a natural part of your daily life. This book is about giving you the tools to do just that – to practice, refine and master affirmative prayer and use it every day to transform your life.

Nothing, and I mean NOTHING, has transformed my life more powerfully than speaking affirmative prayer every day. I often joke that I pray every day, whether I need it or not. The truth is that there is always something to pray about for myself, for my loved ones and for the world. Writing, and eventually speaking, a daily affirmative prayer is a beautiful way to step into a more anchored spiritual practice. And, best of all, it works.

So, let's start at the very beginning. What, exactly, is affirmative prayer? Where does it come from? And how does it work? I would certainly want to know that stuff before I started learning about a new form of spiritual practice. According to Wikipedia, affirmative prayer is a form of prayer or a metaphysical technique that is focused on a positive outcome rather than a negative situation, affirming that the outcome has already happened. You'll notice as you read this book that affirmative prayers are always in the present tense. We are affirming something that is happening now, not that it will happen at some point in the future. (After all, if we affirm that it will happen in the future, it will always stay in the future!) I would add to this definition that affirmative is dynamic, meaning that it brings forth action. We consciously and intentionally use affirmative prayer to change the conditions of our life. We can use it to heal our bodies, grow our bank accounts, mend relationships and so much more. It's a tool we can use to create the lives we have only dreamed of.

In this book, we are focusing on a specific form of Affirmative Prayer called Spiritual Mind Treatment, which is found in the writings of Ernest Holmes. In case you are new to the works of Ernest Holmes, he wrote The Science of Mind, This Thing Called You, and A New Design for Living, among many others. He was a prolific author and teacher, as well as the founder of the philosophy of Religious Science. Centers for Spiritual Living, an international organization of spiritual centers, continues to share the metaphysical philosophy of Dr. Holmes today.

In the spirit of full disclosure, I should tell you that I am a minister with Centers for Spiritual Living. I've studied this particular form of affirmative prayer extensively, and I've used it in every area of my life. If you could interview my friends and family, they'd tell you that years of daily affirmative prayer have shaped me into a calmer, saner, more loving person. They'd tell you that it has given me the confidence to go after big dreams, like getting my Masters Degree and writing this book.

And that, dear reader, is what I want for you. Whatever your big dreams are, I want you to have the faith and the gumption to jump into the abyss and make them happen. Whatever challenges seem to be blocking your way, I want you to melt them away under the Light of Truth. Whatever you want to be that you think is impossible, I want you to discover that you already are. Let's do this thing!

# FOUNDATIONAL ASSUMPTIONS

Affirmative prayer is based on five key ideas, or foundational assumptions, about the Nature of the Divine. Understanding these assumptions will help affirmative prayer make sense to you, which is the first step in embracing the practice of daily prayer. These five key ideas are:

1. God is not a person. Think of it as a Universal Consciousness, an Energy, that flows through everything. It's not a person, so It doesn't have a personality. It's neither a he nor a she, or maybe It's both and more. I prefer to use the word "It" rather than a gendered pronoun. This may be really different than what you're used to, but it makes much more sense than creating God in the likeness and image of us.

2. God is all there is. Everything is made up of It – the mountains, the stars, people --even us. There's nothing supernatural to see here, folks. This is just the way the Universe is built. Since God is all there is, there's nothing else to be made of. Every part of every one of us is God-stuff.

3. Since we're all made up of God-Stuff, we already have within us every attribute needed in order to be and do whatever we want. The Love of God is already within us, as is the Peace of God and the Abundance of God. All of It is already built into us. Now, we may not be accessing those attributes terribly well right now, but the latent qualities are there at the center of who we are.

4. The Highest God and the Innermost God are One God – the same God. That's why, in affirmative prayer, we're not talking to a God out there, asking for things. We're talking to ourselves, reminding ourselves about the Truth of who we are

and why we are that way. (In case you aren't following, who we are is an emanation of God, whole and complete because we are made of God-Stuff.) Affirmative prayer changes us, and because we are all part of the Infinite Oneness that is God, our prayers reach out through that Oneness and touch everyone and everything. With every prayer, we are shifting the consciousness of the Universe. Isn't that amazing?

5. There are many names for God, and they all work. For the rest of this class, I'll use lots of different names. Some of my favorites are: The Beloved One, Sweet Spirit, Universal Mind and Divine Perfection. I have a friend that calls God Howard. It really doesn't matter, as long as it evokes that sense of Universal Divine for you. If I use a name for God that bothers you, just mentally replace that name with one you prefer. Here's a hint: if you see a word capitalized in this book (like Love or Truth), I'm using it as a name for God.

> *"There is a key to right living, a golden key to happiness and success, and this key is in our own thought; it is our affirmative prayer. Such prayer is our direct line of communion with the Invisible. It is through this union that the mind is cleared of negative thoughts, of doubts and fears. This we must do if we are to become aware of the Presence of God within and around us."*
>
> **Ernest Holmes**

# HOW IT WORKS

Most people are a little bit thrown the first few times they hear an affirmative prayer, as it sounds so different than traditional Christian prayer. We've all heard, and probably even spoken, prayers of begging, beseeching and negotiating with an external, distant God. That's not what we're doing here. Instead, affirmative prayer is essentially an organized, logical argument with your own brain. Your old ideas, memories and beliefs about the world (and about yourself) can stop you from having the life you want. The crazy thing is you may not even know they are there! Beliefs like, "People never change," "Nice guys never win," or "I'll never get ahead," might be hiding in your unconscious right now, interfering with your ability to consciously create the life you want. Now, whether you believe in the Law of Attraction (the idea that your thoughts attract corresponding things into your life) or whether you believe these hidden beliefs unconsciously affect your behaviors, it doesn't really matter. Both are probably true, and the end effect is the same. These ideas are getting in your way and affirmative prayer is the best method I've found for letting them go.

The five-step Affirmative Prayer logical argument goes like this:

**Recognition Step:** Spirit is _____ (a whole bunch of stuff that you know that God is, in the form of spiritual qualities). Eternal, All-Knowing, pure Love, absolute Abundance. Sweet Spirit is expressing as everyone and everything. Include whatever matters to you and helps you find that sense of how amazing and huge and powerful Spirit is.

**Unification Step:** I am one with God. I am made up of God stuff, so I am that which God is. I am Love, Prosperity, or whatever qualities you have claimed for God.

**Realization Step:** Because I am the _____ (fill in the blank quality) that God is, I am experiencing (the thing or experience) that I want now. (Note the present tense.)

**Thanksgiving Step:** I am so thankful to know this is already the Truth.
**Release Step:** I release this prayer into the Law – the mechanism of how the Energetic Universe works. Much like God, we use a lot of different descriptive names for the Law, but they all mean essentially the same thing. Throughout this book, you'll find "the Law of Universal Action," "the Law of Cause and Effect" and "the Law of Creative Medium." I like to close the release step of my affirmative prayers with "And So It Is". That's basically what Amen means in modern English. Amen is fine too. My friend Kathleen says, "Yay, God!" Whatever works for you is just dandy.

Affirmative prayer is the single best method I've found to connect with the Divine and change my life. Learning to write and speak affirmative prayers can be a bit daunting at first, I know. The structure can be intimidating, but I wrote this book to make the process easier for you. You can start right where you are. If you are brand new to affirmative prayer, spend some time reading the prayers I've written for you in Chapter Four and witness your life as it begins to transform. If you are ready to start create your own prayers, begin with the *Writing Your Own Affirmative Prayers* section and follow the step-by-step instructions. Everything you need to know to write a customized affirmative prayer is right there. I invite you to write or speak an affirmative prayer every day for a month and you will notice that the words begin to flow.

Here's a quick tip: the affirmative prayers I have provided for you in the *Affirmative Prayer Library* section are specifically written to help you expand your prayer language. I used different words and phrases to start the five steps of each prayer. This offers you.25 ways to begin a Recognition step, 25 ways to begin a Unification step, and so on. Essentially, I wrote the affirmative prayer book I wish I'd had when I was first learning. Feel free to experiment with your language choices and to borrow liberally from what I have written. It's there for you.

I'm so excited for you at this moment in your spiritual journey. As you read, write and speak affirmative prayers, pay attention to the ways your life changes. Notice how your relationships shift, and any differences in the way you feel on the inside. See for yourself if daily affirmative prayer is the spiritual tool you've been missing. I believe that you are going to experience an amazing transformation. After all, real change happens when you put Spirit first.

## Karen's Prayer Experience

***Affirmative prayer is one of the single most powerful tools you can use to transform your life.**
**I used to live in fear, playing small, always choose the safest option, even though this did nothing to feeding my soul's desire. Using daily affirmative prayer, I have been able to radically transform my life to one of freedom and power. Affirmative prayer provided me with an avenue to know my highest and best in all situation. Through this, I've learned how to take the risk and step into my Greatness. I would recommend to anyone looking to have a new experience and know that it will help you to step into the life you were born to live.***

# WRITING YOUR OWN AFFIRMATIVE PRAYERS

The structure of affirmative prayer is one of the most important elements of its power and effectiveness. It can also, however, be a big challenge for those new to this kind of prayer. To make it easier for you to begin, I've created a little cheat sheet – the Affirmative Prayer Template. Located in Chapter Five, the Affirmative Prayer Template lists the steps in order and gives you spaces to fill in each portion of your prayer. I encourage you to make some copies of this template and to use it until you are very, very comfortable with the structure of affirmative prayer. (You can also download a digital version at www.lezligoodwin.com/affirmativeprayer) Anything that makes this process easier for you will make it more likely that you will stick with the daily prayer-writing practice and experience the amazing benefits of affirmative prayer.

NOTE: Using this template is not cheating. Yeah, yeah, I know I called it a cheat sheet in the above paragraph... I've had students tell me that they think they aren't "really writing the prayer" if they use the template. Get over that silliness right now. Use the template. It's not hurting anything, and it's likely helping you have a faster, more connected prayer-writing process. It's good. You're good. We good? Good.

# THE THREE PREP STEPS

The first thing I do when I write an affirmative prayer is to complete three Prep Steps. These Prep Steps help me gain clarity around the prayer I am about to write and set me up for a better prayer-writing experience. These Prep Steps are not a part of what Ernest Holmes taught, but they work beautifully with this system of affirmative prayer. I learned some of this in classes and from various teachers, and some of it I've figured out for myself over the years. What I know is that taking a few moments to go through these quick Prep Steps allows me to write prayers that are clearer, more connected and more powerful.

Our three Preps are called Problem, Quality and Purpose. This process is going to help us zoom in on what, exactly, we are praying for and why.

First, we need to decide what problem we would like this prayer to solve. What would we like to be different in our lives because of this prayer? I invite you to take a moment to close your eyes and take a deep, cleansing breath. Now, allow to rise up in your mind the one thing that is most impacting your personal sense of well-being. It might be a challenged relationship. It might be not having enough money to do something you really want to do. It might be a health issue. Whatever it is, let it be very, very clear in your mind. When you are ready, open your eyes and write your problem under Problem on your Affirmative Prayer Template.

As we go through this process, I'm going to create a sample prayer to illustrate the steps. This way, you will be able to see exactly how the instructions play out in an actual prayer. For my sample prayer, I'm using a situation that is common and relatable: I just got laid off from my job and I am freaking out about money. Whatever problem you're addressing in this prayer should feel very real, because it is! Don't try to sugar coat at this stage. This is not the time for spiritual language and seeing the sunny side. Just get the true feelings out there, in all their messy glory

Now, take a look at the Spiritual Qualities page in Chapter Four. You'll see a whole bunch of qualities listed, like Love, Peace, Abundance, Grace… This page doesn't include every Spiritual Quality, because those qualities are infinite, but it's a really good start. What we're going to do is circle any qualities that feel like they would be helpful in changing the way you feel about your problem.

For example, my problem is "I just got laid off from my job and I'm freaking out about money." When I put the emphasis on "laid off" and "money", it becomes clear that I could really use the spiritual qualities of abundance and prosperity. That sounds really good, right? And when I put the emphasis on "freaking out", I can see that I need the spiritual qualities of Peace and Trust.

Doesn't it make sense that bringing in the spiritual qualities of Peace, Trust, Abundance and Prosperity would be effective in solving my sample problem?

Take a look at the Spiritual Qualities page and identify the qualities that would be most helpful in resolving the problem you've chosen for this prayer. When you are ready, write your quality or qualities under Quality on your Affirmative Prayer Template. Take as much time as you need to feel into which quality or qualities represent a solution to you. This is an essential step that will affect every step of the affirmative prayer you are writing.

Finally, we get to create our Purpose, an affirmation statement about the solution we seek.

We're getting into the nitty gritty now, and there are some very specific requirements for purpose statements. Your purpose statement should use the qualities you've identified. It should be specific about the solution sought. It should be written in the present tense, because we are affirming it's happening right now. If we affirm something will happen in the future, that thing will always stay in the future. Instead, we want to experience this solution right now.

Again, my sample problem is "I just got laid off from my job and I am freaking out about money. A good purpose statement for this problem might be, "I am Peace as I Trust Spirit to demonstrate my Abundance and Prosperity in my new job now." Does it fit the guidelines? Let's check: Does it use my qualities? Yep. Is it specific? Yes, it says exactly how I want to feel and what I want to get – a new job! And is it in the present tense? Yes! It says now.

Now it's your turn! Take a moment and write your purpose statement. Remember the three requirements, so that your purpose statement sets up your prayer to bring you exactly what you want. When you are ready, write your purpose statement on your Affirmative Prayer Template. Not only does this carefully crafted purpose statement prepare you for an awesome prayer, but it also makes an excellent affirmation. Try saying it ten times when you feel stressed out, or post it in a place you regularly see, like your bathroom mirror or your cell phone home screen. Simply by identifying what you want and stating it in a positive way, you are already on your way to having it!

> *"Not everyone has that great faith. I didn't have it. But I learned there is a key, there is a secret—not a mystery. There is a way in which any living soul may consciously reproduce the monumental works of those who have that faith; and the way is through persistent positive prayer."*
>
> *Ernest Holmes*

# STEP ONE: RECOGNITION

Now that we have completed our three Prep Steps, we are ready to dig in to the five steps of affirmative prayer. Keep your Affirmative Prayer Template handy, as we will continue to utilize it through these five steps.

The first step of affirmative prayer is called Recognition. This is the step where we recognize all that Spirit, or God, is. It's really about focusing in on our awe and amazement at the enormity and power of the Divine. It is, truly, all that there is. It knows all. There is nothing It cannot do. And It is always present, in and through all things. Spirit is inherently all of the spiritual qualities we value. It is the Source of all of those qualities. Most importantly for us right now, Spirit is the qualities we have identified in our purpose statement.

This kind of affirmative prayer is pretty structured, so it's worth taking a few moments to cover what we don't talk about in the Recognition Step. We don't talk about anything but the nature of Spirit. That means we don't talk about ourselves at all in this step. We also don't talk about our situation. Instead, we allow all of our energy to be focused on the magnificence of Almighty Spirit, the All-Good.

Now, in my example, I was freaking out about money because I had just been laid off. We had identified the spiritual qualities of Abundance, Prosperity, Peace and Trust as the qualities that would move me from fear into faith and resolution in this situation. So, in my Recognition step, I'm going to describe God in these terms, bringing up ways I see these qualities in God and throughout creation.

The big trick with the Recognition step is to stay with it until you really feel the enormity of the Presence of the Divine well up inside you. That feeling of awe is the cue that you're ready to move to the next step.

So, my Recognition Step might read, "There is only One, one Source of All That Is. Expressing through all things, It is Abundance and Prosperity, forever increasing. It is deep Peace and abiding Trust, the knowingness that all is well. It contains every answer, every solution, every opportunity, supporting all of life perfectly and beautifully."

You might want to include concrete examples of each quality, like the abundance of the countless and uncountable grains of sand on every beach, all over the world. The natural prosperity of animals in the wild, always finding more than enough food and water to keep themselves and their families fed and nourished. They don't go to work to earn that privilege. It is theirs by Divine birthright.

You might talk about the deep Peace of a sweet baby nestled safely in her mother's arms, completely calm and knowing she is safe. Or the perfect Trust of a baby bird as it jumps out of the nest and takes its first flight, inherently knowing that it will be okay. Whatever examples and words you need in order to feel that wonderment of Infinite Good are absolutely perfect. Take as much time as you need to build that energy. You aren't finished with this step until every fiber of your being knows beyond a shadow of a doubt that the God you are talking about is brimming over with the qualities you have identified.

When you are ready, use the Affirmative Prayer Template and write your own Recognition Step using your personal situation and your own identified qualities. Take some time to revel in the feelings that come up. It's an amazing thing to know that everything you need is right here, in Spirit. That knowledge gives us hope, and the energy you're building will be what powers your affirmative prayer.

> *"The principle of effective, affirmative prayer is simply -- The results will always be equal to the inner belief of the one giving the prayer at the time he gives the prayer!"*
>
> *Ernest Holme*

# STEP TWO: UNIFICATION

The second step of affirmative prayer is Unification. This is the step where we recognize that, since God made everything, we are what It is. That means that we have within us everything that we recognized about God in the previous step.

I am made of Spirit, so at the core of my nature, I am everything that Spirit is.

If this is difficult for you, think of it this way: Legos are hard and plastic. They have flat, smooth sides. They have bumps on the top and have openings on the bottom. They are colorful. These are the qualities of Lego blocks.

Photo Credit: istockphoto.com/ekaterina79

Lego buildings are made up of Lego blocks. A Lego building looks really different from a pile of Lego blocks, but it has to have the same qualities. Let's check and see if it's right. Lego buildings are hard and plastic. Check. Lego buildings have flat, smooth sides. Check, look at the edge of that wall – a flat, smooth side. Lego bumps have bumps on the top and openings on the bottom. Yep, when I look at the yellow construction pieces and the grass, I can see the bumps. When I look at the red block the two Lego construction guys are carrying, I can see the openings on the bottom that can be connected to bumps. Lego buildings are colorful. Check – I see red, yellow, blue, green... lots of colors. It's true. A Lego building has the same qualities as Lego blocks, because it is made up of them. Does that make sense?

Photo Credit: istockphoto.com/meskolo

In the Unification step, we talk about how I am one with The One. I am made up of God-stuff. Therefore, I am all of the qualities that I recognize in God. Hard, plastic, wait, no.... That's Legos! God shows up as qualities like love, grace, wholeness, abundance, joy, goodness and so much more. Those same qualities exist in me in full potential, whether I am seeing or using them right now or not.

Returning to my example, we recall that I was freaking out about money because I had just been laid off. We had identified the spiritual qualities of Abundance, Prosperity, Peace and Trust as the qualities that would move me from fear into faith and resolution in this situation. In our Recognition step, we Recognized that The Source is Abundance, Prosperity, Peace and Trust in Its nature. So, in my Unification step, I'm going to describe how I am one with my Source, so I contain these same qualities.

Just like with the Recognition step, it's really important to stay with the Unification step until it feels absolutely true. The rest of the prayer builds on this sense of certainty.

So, my Unification Step might read: As I am made in the image of That Which Made Me, I am that which It is. There's nothing else for me to be, because God is all there is! I am abundance and prosperity. I am deep peace and abiding trust. The truth of my nature is Divine. It is imprinted on my very DNA. I have access to all things good.

You will see that I used the very same qualities in this step that I used in the Recognition step. It may sound a little repetitive, but that's okay. There's an old marketing adage that says you have to see something seven times before you believe it. Repeating the qualities is actually going to help deepen your faith in the truth of your prayers. As you work your way through the steps of affirmative prayer, you're building your logical argument.

Remember, affirmative prayer is essentially an organized, logical argument with your own brain. We're building the argument that because God is Abundance, Prosperity, Peace and Trust, and because God made me, I have to be Abundance, Prosperity, Peace and Trust in my nature. Even if I'm not accessing or experiencing those qualities right now, they are within me awaiting activation. Take some time now to utilize the Affirmative Prayer Template and write your own Unification Step using your personal situation and your own identified qualities.

# STEP THREE: REALIZATION

The Third step of affirmative prayer is Realization. You may have noticed that we haven't asked for anything in our affirmative prayer thus far. We haven't mentioned the things we would like to have or experience in any way. In the third step, we have the opportunity to address the condition we would like to see differently. In other words, we have arrived at the place in affirmative prayer where we address the Problem and Purpose Prep Steps. And, of course, there is a specific structure that we follow.

In affirmative prayer, we address the changes we would like to see in, well, an affirmative way. There is no begging and no bargaining. Instead, Realization is the step where we claim and affirm that whatever solution, resolution or experience we'd like to have is already here for us. We essentially Realize that, since we already have within us the qualities needed to resolve our situation, the thing we want is already available right where we are.

This is why we've been talking about those "solution" qualities in the Recognition and Unification steps. At this point, it should flow naturally and logically that since Spirit is (fill in the blank quality), and Spirit made me to be like It, I am (quality). Since (quality) is what's needed to solve my situation, of course I already have the solution. It should be a *DUH! No-brainer* proposition.

Here's the important thing. If you get to this point and it doesn't feel like a foregone conclusion that you already have access to everything you need for the Purpose of your prayer, you need to go back to the Recognition step and begin again. You'll remember that we talked about staying with each step until you feel fully convinced of the truth of your words. This is why that was important. When you have fully assimilated the first two steps, the third step is really easy. If you haven't fully assimilated the first two steps, the third step us nearly impossible. I mean, it's easy to say the words. You just may not believe them.

Let's talk about what goes in the Realization step:

I like to begin this step with "And so I speak my Word". Notice how I capitalized "Word"? That's because I'm not talking about a word I say. I'm talking about the Word of God, as in "The Word" in John 1:1 "In the beginning was the **Word**, and the **Word** was with God, and **the Word was God**." Because we are expressions of God, when we pray we are speaking the Word of God. That's what makes it so powerful!

(If you find yourself doubting that statement, here is my question for you: If the word you speak is not the Word of God, who's word is it? God is all there is, there's no other kind of word for it to be... Just ponder that for a while and see if you come around to my way of thinking...)

Back to the affirmative prayer... And so I speak my Word for... and here's where I state affirmations about what I want to experience, making sure to use the qualities from my previous two steps. I like to use phrases such as:

- "I affirm that the Love that I already am shows up for me as a wonderful new relationship."

- "The Peace within me is now activated powerfully as a calm, serene sense of wellbeing."

- "Because I am an expression of the Divine, I feel the Grace of God pouring over me, soothing every hurt feeling like a healing balm."

These phrases are a continuation of the logical argument I have been having with my brain, and in this step, I win the argument. There is no doubt that I can have the change I am seeking, because that change flows directly from a quality that Spirit Itself built into me. The Truth makes Itself known in my prayer and in my life.

Affirmative Prayer is always in the present tense (it's happening now), but this step is where it can be tempting to put things in future tense. As in, "I will meet a wonderful person and our relationship will be beautiful." Nope. A wonderful person appears to me now and our relationship is beautiful. There can be a bit of a temptation to look around, not see a person, and say "No, that's not true." But remember, that which we affirm for the future always stays in the future. The truth is that, right in the moment you speak your Word, a chain of events is set in motion that is bringing that person to you. We don't know how many events are in that chain or how long it will be before you actually see that person, but the events are already unfolding before you even finish the prayer.

This is the step where you get to be specific. Yes, you want a relationship. But you may specifically want a committed romantic relationship with a man who is funny, kind and loving. Go ahead and claim what you want! I do encourage you to be careful about being so specific that it limits your good – for example, you might not want to say, "I claim a committed romantic relationship with Steve Johnson, the married man that lives next door." Or "I claim a committed romantic relationship with a 6'4" tall white man with brown hair and green eyes, who is a generous billionaire, fifteen years younger than me, in world class shape, owns his own plane which he flies himself, has been nominated for a Nobel Prize at least once and knows Oprah personally." I'm not saying those prayers won't work. I'm just saying that a broader description of what you want will be more likely to manifest in your life more quickly and with fewer problems along the way. (Steve Johnson's wife, for example, might not appreciate the unfoldment of your prayer!) The Universe responds more quickly and more powerfully when it has more paths to your Good!

Finally, this is the place where we get to uproot and toss out any false beliefs we have about ourselves, about our prayer topic or about the nature of the Universe. If we haven't manifested what we want before this moment, there may be something in our consciousness that is saying "No" to our good. In our relationship example, maybe I am thinking deep down that I don't deserve a great, loving guy. Or maybe a tiny part of me is afraid of getting hurt, or thinks all the good men are taken. I've got to let that belief go, or it could interfere with my prayer!

Remember in the *All About Affirmative Prayer* section, we talked about the Law always accepting the impress of our thoughts and manifesting them? Yeah, unfortunately, that's true of our negative thoughts and beliefs! So, this step is a great place to let go of those false negative ideas. I like to use phrases like, "And so I release any and all thoughts or beliefs that have kept me from my perfect, loving relationship, for they are not the Truth!"

That way, even if I'm not clear on exactly what has held me back, I can know that God is working on my mind and heart to open me up in a new way.

Returning once again to my example: I was freaking out about money because I had just been laid off. We had identified the spiritual qualities of Abundance, Prosperity, Peace and Trust as the qualities that represented a solution to my current condition. We had affirmed that since God is those qualities, I am those same qualities. Moving into the third step,

My Realization Step might read:  And so, I speak my Word now for my financial life, realizing that The Divine is already at work for my highest Good.  I affirm that the Abundance that I already am is making itself known as the perfect new job for me, right here and right now.  This job fits my skills beautifully, and utilizes my creativity, intelligence and communication abilities.  Tapping into my Divine Prosperity, this job is wonderfully compensated, bringing me more than enough financial good to meet all of my obligations, have room for some luxury and still have plenty left over to tithe and give to charity.  I am Peace and Trust at the core of my being, believing and knowing that The All-Good is already calling forth this wonderful job, in which I am powerfully supported by management and given room to grow and expand.  I release, right now in this moment, any and all thoughts, ideas or patterns of belief that have kept me from my perfect, wonderful job and my overflowing financial good.  They were never the Truth and they have no Power, for only God has Power in my life! My heart is calm, knowing powerfully that I am completed supported and supplied by The One Which Made All Things.  All is well, right here and right now.

At this point, everything in my being is saying, "YES!" to this prayer, knowing absolutely that it is so. I've made my logical argument, and my entire heart is completely aligned with my Good.

Now it's your turn to utilize the Affirmative Prayer Template and write your own Realization Step using your personal situation and your own identified qualities.  Build upon your work in the Recognition and Unification Steps to claim and affirm the changes you are ready to call forth through this prayer.

# STEP FOUR: THANKSGIVING

The Fourth step of affirmative prayer is Thanksgiving. This is the step where we get to express our gratitude and grateful thanks that what we have wanted and affirmed and claimed throughout the prayer is already true.

"But wait", you may say, "I don't see that new relationship yet! How can I be thankful for it?" We are filled with thanks because we recognize that the Word we have already spoken is already so in the One Mind of God. And since everything emanates from the One Mind, what's so in It MUST come into manifest physical form. In other words, what's true in the Mind of God has to become real in the world – that's just the way the Law (or the energetic rules of the Universe) works. You might have heard the Hermetic phrase, "As above, so below." It means what is true in the Divine realm has to come forth in the Earthly realm. That's just a bunch of different ways of saying the same thing – what's true in God has to be true here in the world, even if we don't see the evidence quite yet. And, as we impress our thoughts (or, our Word) into the Law, we are calling out what part of the infinitude of the Truth in God's Mind we'd like to see in our world now. So, we can be filled with thanks, knowing that Good is rushing to us right now. It's a fact!

Now, an interesting thing about this step is that we are NOT thanking God for our Good. Yep, you heard that correctly. We are not thanking God for our prayer coming true. And here's why – We haven't asked God for anything. That's not what affirmative prayer is about. Affirmative prayer is about Recognizing what is already true about God and about ourselves, and then Realizing what that means for our life now. It's about claiming what part of that infinite Truth we'd like to experience at this time and knowing that, once that preference is placed powerfully into the Law of Divine Action, that preference has to manifest for us. There's no asking, pleading, begging, beseeching or hoping in there. You may notice that there is no earning, deserving or hoping for worthiness in there, either. We are all inherently worthy of whatever we desire, as long as it is positive and doesn't hurt anyone. Why are we worthy? Because we are emanations of The One, made up of God-Stuff and created in the likeness and image of God Itself. So, we don't have to thank a being for giving us gifts. We simply are thankful, recognizing the powerful Good and celebrating it as it hurries to us in physical form. In some of his writings, Ernest Holmes called this step Acceptance, which in some ways is a better name.

Let's talk about what goes in the Thanksgiving step. I like to include phrases like, "I give grateful thanks," "I am filled with gratitude," or "My heart sings with thankfulness." Why am I thankful? For whatever thing, and more importantly quality, I prayed for being manifest in my life right now! "For Love as my perfect, wonderful romantic relationship," or "for my amazing new job and all the Abundance it brings me," or even just "because I know the Word I have spoken is already true in the Mind of God." Just let yourself really feel that gratitude, and let it be in the present tense. That Good is here now, not in some future time. Right now.

So, getting back to my example, I was freaking out about money because I had just been laid off. We had identified the spiritual qualities of Abundance, Prosperity, Peace and Trust as the qualities that represented a solution to my current condition. We had affirmed that since God is those qualities, I am those same qualities and get to experience those qualities in my life now.

So, my Thanksgiving Step might read: My heart is overflowing with profound gratitude at the powerful knowingness that my perfect job is here, right now. I give grateful, grateful thanks for the Abundance and Prosperity manifesting in my life right at this moment. I am thankful for my deep sense of Peace and Trust. All is well in the Universal Mind, and so I know all is well in my life, and it is good!

At this point in the prayer, my heart is just bursting with joy and gratitude for all of the amazing goodness in my life! I am thankful for the way the Law works. I am thankful for knowing about the nature of God, and that I am a part of It. I'm pretty much thankful for everything! It's a really, really good feeling, and this heart opening sensation is a really good indicator of how effective your prayer will be. If you get to this point in the prayer and you're not feeling awesome, it's time to take a moment and think about what's missing. Have you hurried through the steps, putting in the right elements but not taking the time to allow the feelings to build?

Is a part of your brain still arguing that what you're saying can't be true? Only you can know what needs more work to have the experience you want. Once you give yourself the time and space to let your prayer develop, the natural gratitude will come. It's a pretty overwhelming feeling to know that the Power of the Almighty is working on your behalf in every moment! As you utilize the Affirmative Prayer Template to write your own Thanksgiving Step, see if you can connect to that profound sense of gratitude and awe.

> *"We proceed on the theory that there is a Divine Presence in everything and everyone, and that this Presence responds to us. Our recognition of this, our acceptance of it, our prayer of affirmation causes a response to us in a new way. This is a new manifestation that rises to the level of our expectation, our faith, our conviction, and our inner acceptance."*
>
> *Ernest Holmes*

# STEP FIVE: RELEASE

Release is the fifth and final step of affirmative prayer. This is the step where we "let go and let God". It's really a step of trust, a step of remembering that we don't have to make the prayer manifest. It will simply come into form as a means of the Law doing what the Law always does, by reflecting back to us what we have thought or spoken into it. If we've done our part properly – claiming what we want and understanding why we can have it, as well as releasing any false beliefs about why we couldn't have it – then it's an absolute no-brainer at this point that our prayer is manifesting right now.

It's important to release the prayer, because trust and faith are all about getting out of the way and letting the Law do Its thing. I love the old example from the garden: We plant a seed (our thought or Word) into the fertile soil (the Law). We water it and give it sunshine (affirmations, belief, faith). We know how seeds grow, and that it takes some time for that little green sprout to poke up through the ground. If we dig into the earth every day to check on its progress, the plant will never have a chance to grow. We have to leave it alone and trust that it is making its way up into the sunshine where we can see it. Affirmative prayers are very much the same. We water the prayer faithfully with our knowingness and trust that the manifestation is coming to us. If we let doubt sneak in, we're digging up the soil. When I catch myself doubting, I do another affirmative prayer – that's me, being a good gardener. And then I do my best to LEAVE IT ALONE! The Law, once it has our Word, doesn't need our help to make it happen!

To complete my example: I was freaking out about money because I had just been laid off. We had identified the spiritual qualities of abundance, prosperity, peace and trust as the qualities that represented a solution to my current condition. We had affirmed that since God is those qualities, I am those same qualities. I get to experience those qualities in my life now and I am thankful.

So, my Release Step might read: I release my Word into the action of Universal Law, knowing it is already done. I trust completely that it is already true in the Mind of God, and so it is rushing to me in manifest form right now! I let it be, with complete faith. And so it is!

There is nothing in this world that compares to the feeling of a completed affirmative prayer. The overwhelming relief and peace that comes with the Releasing Step can bring me to tears. What a joy it is to know that the entire Universe is conspiring to bring me my Good, simply because I have placed my Word into the Law. God is so Good! It really is amazing. And yet, it's happening with every thought of our lives, whether we realize it or not. Every thought, every belief, goes straight into the Law. Affirmative prayer just gives us a structure to help us place what we consciously WANT into the Law and have a life that is powerfully aligned with our desires.

As you write your customized Release Step, take a moment to reflect back on all that you've learned. Through the process of writing this affirmative prayer, you've recognized and aligned with Divine Truth. You've realized that all that you desire is already present for you, and you've felt profound gratitude. Now, as you release your prayer into the Law of Universal Action, you are trusting the entire Universe to conspire for your very highest and best, knowing that it is so.

You now fully understand how to write customized affirmative prayers whenever you need them. I'm so excited that you have mastered this fabulous tool to transform your life. Just imagine how it will be, now that you have this structure to release any thoughts or beliefs that no longer serve you and to claim everything you want in a powerful way! I can't wait to see what unfolds for you! It is going to be AMAZING!

> *"When we turn our prayer over to the Law, we are setting cause and effect in motion."*
>
> **Ernest Holmes**

## Sandra's Prayer Experience

*When my life partner died, I had to consider my future and that included where I would live. I owned a rental house in Chandler that had been my home. Returning there seemed like a step into the past, instead of a step into a new life. Staying in Mesa was not an option. I wanted to be closer to my spiritual home at New Vision Center as well as other activities in Phoenix. I targeted Tempe and Scottsdale. Next came my idea of what kind of home I wanted. Being retired I wanted to travel and enjoy myself. I wanted to be free to explore, write, dance, hike. In short, I wanted easy living and having fun. Lawn care, gardening did not fit my plan. Besides, I wanted to find somewhere I could age in place.*

*I created an image of the perfect house. Open floor plan, three bedrooms, walk-in closet, two-car garage, desert landscape, nice patio.*

*I held this image in my mind as I worked with a real estate agent to find my new home. Nothing that fit my budget, nor my vision turned up in the chosen area. So, we expanded the search. The first house I visited exactly matched the image I had created and was less than my top price. Not only that, the house was even better than what I imagined with lots of upgrades and extra features. The Phoenix location put me closer to NVC and my other activities.*

*My prayers were answered!*

*This experience taught me the importance of having clear goals and a specific image of what I wanted to manifest and why. In addition, it taught me patience, persistence and the amazing gift of receiving more than I requested. Now if I can apply this lesson to all other aspects of my life, no telling what my future will hold!*

# TAKING THINGS FURTHER

Okay, you have learned how to write beautiful, customized affirmative prayers. You've got the structure and flow down pat. Good for you! Now what? Knowing how to write affirmative prayers won't do you any good unless you actually pray. The knowledge and understanding, without action, can't change your life. Here are some tried and true ways to deepen and strengthen your prayer life and put your affirmative prayers into action.

## DAILY PRAYER, WHETHER YOU NEED IT OR NOT

There is a conversation that I have with nearly every student as they learn to use Affirmative Prayer in their lives. "How often do I need to do this," they will ask. "Once a month? Once a week?" Students are almost always startled by my answer, "Every day, whether you need it or not."

Of course, I'm kidding. Not about the *every day* part – no, I'm deadly serious about that. I'm joking about the idea that a day might come when there is no need for affirmative prayer. The challenge is that, in Western culture, we're conditioned to not ask for much. Many affirmative prayer students are reluctant to pray for themselves, especially when it's not a life or death situation. Some are reticent to pray for abundance or success. Some resist the idea that they should place their intention into the Law, but should instead allow "God's Will" to be done without interference. There are many reasons to avoid daily affirmative prayer, but the spiritual Truth overcomes all excuses and confusions.

**It's Selfish to Pray for My Good:** A left-over idea from guilt-based and fear-based religions, the idea that it is selfish to want good things in your life is simply false. After all, God is literally the All-Good, and we are made in Its image. As expressions of this perfect God, we already contain the seeds of every form of Good. It just makes sense that our lives be expanding expressions of the All-Goodness of the Divine in every single way. Our primary charge as a human being is to reveal as much God-ness as we possibly can in this life, which makes it our job to call forth as much Good as possible. Doing what God asks of us can never be a selfish thing. So, go ahead and claim your Good!

**I Should Only Pray for Important Things:** While I can understand this sentiment, it has some logical flaws. First, every intention is released into the Law and comes into manifest form in the same. The Law is immune to the ideas of size, importance and amount. It is the same process to heal cancer as it is to heal a paper cut, if it's placed into the Law believing. There are no bonus points for the size or importance of the request. Second, this concern implies that God answers some prayers and not others depending on its perceived importance. Everything placed into the Law with belief brings a response proportional to the belief. We can't use up God's Love on the little prayers and risk It not being willing to help when the big stuff comes. That's simply not how it works. Spirit is infinite.

**It's Greedy to Pray for Money:** Even when people move past the concern about praying for their own Good, often a fear about praying for money remains. Here is what I want you to know – Abundance is a God quality. It is a spiritual Truth that we are all made in the likeness and image of Spirit Itself, and that we are each imbued with Its qualities. If The Divine built the quality of Abundance into you, how could it be harmful or sinful to activate and utilize that quality? It can't. Simply pray for the Abundance that you already are to call forth more than you need. After all, we do say that God's Grace is my sufficiency in all things, and that includes financial supply.

**I Don't Want to Go Against God's Will:** As we look around at what is going on in our lives, it can be tempting to think, "Well, this must be the way it's supposed to be. It must be God's Will." While I appreciate the sentiment, it's a bit of a cop-out. There is a difference between surrendering into the Divine Guidance of God and just passively allowing life to happen to you. God gave us free will, the Freedom to choose, for a reason. While Spirit is always with us, guiding us to our highest and best, we are called upon to be active in our own lives. Praying for the God qualities we desire to show up more powerfully in our lives can never be against God's will for us, or we wouldn't have been given the Freedom to do so.

**Everything Is Going Great. There's Nothing to Pray For:** This one cracks me up, but it's one of the most common things I hear. Have you ever had a supervisor that only talked to you when you've done something wrong or wanted you to do even more? It's disheartening, right? It would have meant a lot to hear a bit of gratitude for all the things you had done well that day. When we express gratitude and recognition of something good, it brightens the day for both the giver and the receiver. We can't dishearten God, thank goodness, but we are cheating ourselves out of that expanded experience of Good when we forget to pray about the positive things. "Yes, and more please," is one of the best prayers I know! Our moments of awareness when everything that is right are powerful faith builders, and they help us understand what is possible in life.

**Wonderful Affirmative Prayer Opportunities that We Tend to Forget:**
- Before Meetings
- Before Family Events
- Upon Receiving Good News
- When Launching New Projects
- When Leaving on a Trip
- When Feeling Overwhelmed

- When Looking for Ideas or Solutions
- When Seeing an Accident or Emergency
- When Feeling Unsure of the Next Step
- During Times of Relationship Challenge
- When Watching the News
- When Overwhelmed by Gratitude and Love

*"There are occasions when one gives a better or more effective prayer than at other times. This is because it is the inner spiritual awareness back of the prayer that is the motivating power, and at times our faith or spiritual conviction is stronger than at other times."*

*Ernest Holmes*

# PRAYING OUT LOUD

When I first started learning about affirmative prayer, I was encouraged by my teachers to speak the prayers out loud. Oh man, was there RESISTANCE! There was no way I wanted to do that! I worried that people would hear me and think I was weird. I was startled by the sound of my own voice. I felt awkward listening to myself and cringed as I searched for the right words. I wish I had known then that the resistance was normal. Almost everyone feels a little strange about speaking affirmative prayers aloud at first, but there are some really good reasons we encourage it. Once I understood those reasons, it became a little easier for me to step outside of my comfort zone. Isn't that always the way? So, I offer you here the logic behind speaking affirmative prayers out loud in the hopes that it eases your entry into this deepening practice.

**Keeps you Focused on your Prayer:** Affirmative prayers can be kind of long, have many parts and are filled with delicious and delightful imagery. I can't tell you how many times I have started Step One in my head and wandered off into the land of "GOD IS SO AWESOME!", never to return to finish the prayer. When we are saying our prayer silently in our mind, there really isn't anything anchoring us to the structure of affirmative prayer. Recognition of the goodness of Spirit feels so good, we can forget what we were doing in the first place. Luckily, there is nothing bad or wrong about spending time contemplating the profound power of the Divine. No harm, no foul. But what we aren't accomplishing when we lose track of ourselves is practicing affirmative prayer. We aren't getting better at working within the structure. We aren't learning to connect the goodness of God to the goodness present in our own lives right now. We aren't making the power of Spirit concrete and relevant in our own personal situation.

When we speak affirmative prayers out loud, the sound of our voice keeps us focused on the task at hand. We are less likely to slide into a diffuse reverie of fluffy God thoughts. Interestingly, the bit of discomfort that our resistance holds can be an encouragement to push through to the end of the prayer. When the prayer is complete, we get to stop talking out loud! Over time, as we listen, we will notice that our prayers are getting stronger. We struggle less to remember the steps. The language is more fluid and varied. There is more emotion in our voice as we speak the prayers. We find that the time spent really focusing on the prayers has paid off big time.

**Fire in the Belly:** One of the biggest challenges with affirmative prayer is moving from the intellectual space into the heart. While we are keeping track of steps and processes, it's harder to really feel the prayer. And yet, Ernest Holmes, the founder of this teaching, was very clear – it's the emotion, the passion, the fire in the belly that propels the prayer forward. If we want to manifest something, we must have the powerful conviction that the prayer is already done.

It's a curious thing that the exact thing that causes initial discomfort, speaking a prayer out loud, can also be the very element that makes a prayer successful. While we are thinking a prayer in our mind, we might include all the steps and have the ideal wording, but no fire. When we speak an affirmative prayer out loud, though, we are much more likely to allow the feelings to arise and carry us away in the passion of belief. When I am speaking a prayer, I have a tendency to go a little Baptist preacher – eyes closed, arms a-swinging in grand gestures, volume rising as I declare that, "I know that I know that I KNOW!" And I do know, because it's that very feeling, that very fire in the belly, that is the power that pushes my prayer into the Law and brings it into manifestation.

The exciting thing about this is that what makes my affirmative prayers work is something you can do today, right now. I didn't say that my prayers are effective because I've studied for decades. I didn't say that my prayers manifest because my words are perfect. No, my prayers are powerful because of the feeling of belief that I convey. Even if your affirmative prayers aren't perfect yet, you can tap into that deep belief within you at this very moment. You can move from the intellect into the gut feeling that Spirit has your back and it is done unto you as you believe.

**Whole Brain Activity:** A third reason we encourage people to speak their affirmative prayers out loud has to do with the way we receive and process information. As we say a prayer aloud, we are interacting with the prayer three different ways: thinking it, saying it and hearing it. The fields of neuroscience and education have both shown us that, in order to learn and embody information, we should engage as many areas of the brain as possible. As we think up the words we will use, we are stimulating one portion of the brain. As we actually say the words of the prayer, we are activating another area. As we hear the words coming out of our mouths, we are using yet another part. One could reasonably ascertain that using hand motions or movements of some kind would utilize a fourth area. The more segments of the brain we utilize, the more completely we are able to accept that the prayer is true. As we engage our whole brain in an affirmative prayer, we get the benefit of three prayers in one.

With so many benefits to speaking your affirmative prayers out loud, it becomes easier to release any discomfort or nervousness. I remember thinking, "Anyone who knows me already knows I'm weird. This is not going to shock them," and it's true. If anyone hears you, they will likely just be curious. And as your life changes for the better, that curiosity is going to grow. The time will come when people are asking you what's different about you, as they feel your light shining brighter, all because you let yourself feel a little fire in the belly.

*"Whenever prayer becomes meditation and meditation becomes transmuted into acceptance, there is always a demonstration."*

*Ernest Holmes*

# PRAYING FOR SOMEONE ELSE

As you get more and more comfortable with using affirmative prayer, an amazing thing will happen. Your life will begin to change, and people will notice. They won't know what is causing the shift, but it will catch their interest. Why are you suddenly happier? Why are you more successful and productive? Why are you making progress toward your big goal after a decade of dancing on the sidelines? Eventually, after much curiosity and secretive discussions over high-priced lattes, someone will do the unimaginable and will actually ask you. "What is different about you these days?" What they REALLY want to ask is, "Can you help me make the same changes?" And, as quickly as that, you'll find yourself called to speak affirmative prayers for others.

I am always surprised when people are nervous to pray for others. There seems to be a belief that you have to be a Licensed Practitioner of Religious Science or a Prayer Coach to be able to help someone through affirmative prayer. That's just nonsense. Yes, those folks are specially trained and are (of course) particularly good at praying – but anyone can learn. All prayer is good prayer. We're all rowing in the same direction. So, don't sweat it if you are relatively new to this whole scene. With just a few considerations, you can still make a difference for the people in your life that are open and willing.

**Free Will:** When praying for others, the most essential concern is that you not violate the free will of another person. Fortunately, the most common scenario in which you will find yourself praying for someone else is when they ask you to pray for them. In this case, you don't need to worry about praying for something they don't want, as they will give you a specific request.

It can be a little bit more complicated if a friend asks you to pray for someone else (for example, their mother), or if you see something out in the world that calls you to prayer (such as a car accident, or the news). In these circumstances, you can't know either the preference or the path of the person you will be praying for. Depending on the person, even receiving a prayer from someone not of their faith might be a violation! There is a path forward, but it requires caution and awareness.

**Your Friend's Mother:** Imagine that your good friend approaches you and asks you to pray for his mother, who is experiencing some physical challenges. He asks that you pray for her complete and total healing, and that she be free from any disease. This may feel like a pretty easy ask – everyone wants to be healthy, well and free from disease, right? Well, it's not that simple.

The first thing to ask is if his mother has asked for, or is even aware of, the prayer. As I mentioned above, some people are very particular about the kinds of prayers that are spoken on their behalf. While it can be a challenge to understand the logic behind denying a prayer, it's a primary value in spirituality to honor every person's chosen path. Often, you will get a response like, "No, but she's cool with spiritual stuff," or, "No, but she has said she'll take all the good vibes she can get." In situations where it is highly likely that the person would be accepting of a prayer, I generally proceed with caution.

The second thing to look at is the prayer request topic itself. I would recommend asking your friend if she has specifically said she wants a physical healing, a cure or any other particular thing. Despite our sense otherwise, many people don't make such a clear request. They often say things like, "I just want to be better," or "I just want this to be over." I know it's hard to imagine, but not everyone wants a full physical healing. They might be ready to die. They might be getting something out of the illness on a level that we can't be aware of. The disease may be a part of their path that we can't discern. Indeed, they might not even know about it on a conscious level. Our job is simply to step in and speak the prayer that is requested by the individual, not to decide what they should want.

As it is essential to avoid violating someone's free will by praying for something that they haven't explicitly asked for, it is usually best to default to a very high-level prayer that leaves the specifics up to the Intelligence of Spirit. My favorite is, "I affirm and know that the very highest and best is unfolding for Mary right here and right now. Spirit is at work in her mind, body and soul." Isn't that lovely? And it leaves Mary's path to those who have a say – Spirit and Mary.

Finally, I encourage you to ask your friend how he wants to feel about the entire situation. You may not be able to pray in specific detail for his mom, but you absolutely can be specific for your friend. By wrapping him into the prayer, calling forth qualities like Peace, Love or Wisdom in how he supports his mother through this healing process, you can expand the net of Good that you are casting with your prayer.

Your Realization Step might sound like:

"And so, I speak my Word for Jeremy and his mother, Mary. For Mary, I affirm and know that Spirit is at work in her mind, her body and her soul. The very highest and best is unfolding for here right here and now in every single way. I speak a word of blessing over every medical professional, every family member and everyone she has contact with. For Jeremy, I know the profound Peace and Calm of the Divine. I affirm that Jeremy is pure Love and Joy in his relationship with his mother, and that he is the Faith of God in knowing the Truth of Wholeness for All."

Can you see how this prayer addresses your friend's concerns without stomping on the free will of his mother? It takes a bit of thought, but we can absolutely write affirmative prayers that are satisfying and helpful, while also being respectful of those who are not able to share their preferences.

**Victims of a Car Accident:** For this scenario, imagine that you drive by a car accident on the side of the road. There is significant damage, and you feel compelled to pray for the people involved in the accident. This is a good thing, as it shows that you have compassion and loving-kindness for all people. However, we do need to be aware that we don't know if the people in the accident would be open to affirmative prayer or what they would ask for. We are always, always, always careful to protect the free will of every person.

So, how do we pray for these folks who don't even know we're there, let alone that we are praying for them? This is where the ubiquitous "Love and Light" comes in, joining our favorite "highest and best." They may sound like a fluffy bunny cop out, but in my mind they are spiritual shorthand for, "Okay, Spirit. You know the heart and soul of this person in a way I never can. You figure it out and call forth the very best possible path that meets the needs and goals of this person. And hey, if they don't want this prayer, just pass it on to the next person who really needs and wants it."

Your Realization Step might sound like:

"And so, I speak my word for everyone involved in this accident, as well as their families and loved ones. I know that Spirit is right where they are. I affirm that they are each surrounded by Love and Light, and that the highest and best is unfolding for each person. I speak a word of blessing over each rescue and medical professional, trusting that all is well right here and right now."

**Confidentiality:** Whenever we are invited into someone's prayer life, we are given access to their most intimate and sacred secrets. Their fears, their problems, these are things that most people don't share openly. They are putting their faith in us. It is tremendously important that we hold every word absolutely confidential. It is much like a counseling or ministerial role, where a violation of confidentiality can cost you your job. Certainly, a violation of the confidentiality of your prayer relationship will cost you the trust of the person you have harmed. This is our most sacred duty, and you must take it very, very seriously.

**Weird Requests:** You are going to get a reputation for being awesome at praying for people. This is cool, good job you, but it comes with a small challenge. Sometimes, people who are from a different belief system will ask you to pray for them. And while the word "affirmative" should be a tip-off, people don't always ask for the most positive of things. I have received prayer requests like:

- Make my ex-husband fat and miserable.
- Make my lover leave her husband and be with me.
- Help me win the court case against my sister.
- I want my boss fired. (And then I want her job.)

See why I put so much emphasis on the free will thing earlier? Of course, we would never pray for something negative to happen to someone.

We don't even pray for good things to happen to someone without their permission.

There may even be times when the requests are so far removed from New Thought spiritual beliefs that it seems a little odd that they came to you. I've had requests like:

- Make my partner accept Jesus as his Lord and savior.
- Pray that the Devil doesn't have influence over me.
- Save me from the demon living in my body.

The way we handle all of these interesting requests is the same way we handle typical prayer requests. Just like we did for ourselves in the chapter "Writing Your Own Affirmative Prayers," we help the person identify the quality of God they are really seeking. Then, we pray for that quality.

Here's a completely fictitious dialog for you to enjoy:

**GRANT:** Lezli, would you be willing to pray for me? I really need some help.

**LEZLI:** Of course, Grant! Any time! What can I pray for you?

**GRANT:** Well, this might sound a little crazy, but my neighbor put a curse on me and now everything is going wrong in my life! I want you to pray for her to die so the curse will be broken.

*(Interjection: It can be tempting to get side-tracked here and try to find out why he thinks he's cursed, what the deal is with the neighbor, what the "curse" is causing, why he thinks the neighbor dying will break the curse... Resist the urge! You don't need to know any of that to speak the prayer.)*

**LEZLI:** That sounds really challenging, Grant. I'm sorry to hear you're going through all of that. Let me ask you this – What does all of this feel like to you?

**GRANT:** Oh, man, I feel trapped and like I'm constantly under attack!

**LEZLI:** I can really see how it could feel that way. That doesn't sound fun at all. So, I wonder, if the curse was broken right now, how would that feel? Like, imagine it. What does that feel like?

**GRANT:** Relief! It would feel like I am safe.
**LEZLI:** Would it feel like Freedom?

**GRANT:** Oh my God, yes.

**LEZLI:** And would you feel at Peace?

**GRANT:** Yeah, for the first time in so long. I want to feel that.

**LEZLI:** So, you know I speak a special form of prayer called affirmative prayer. Because it's affirmative, we focus on the positive aspects and affirm that the good stuff shows up in your life.

**GRANT:** It will be a good thing in my life when my neighbor dies.

**LEZLI:** Be that as it may, I'd love for you to try it this way. After all, do you really want your neighbor to die? Or do you want to feel Freedom and Peace?

**GRANT:** Both. But I want Freedom and Peace more.

And then I pray for Freedom and Peace. I'd probably toss in a dash of the protection of the Divine for good measure. Maybe I'd mention that nothing can separate Grant from his good. But I wouldn't bring up the neighbor at all. She's not the point. The Divine Truth of Grant is the point. And no matter where the prayer request begins, we can always bring it back to Spiritual Truth.

## *TECHNICAL CONSIDERATIONS*

We've spent most of this book talking about the structure of affirmative prayers you speak for yourself. When we pray for other people, we build upon that foundation but there are a few additional things to take into consideration. The cool thing is that these extra concerns just help us to understand the whys and what-fores of affirmative prayer more completely, inherently improving every prayer we speak.

**Speak in the Third Person:** First, through the entire prayer, we speak in the third person. We don't use the word "you". Instead, we use the person's name or their preferred pronoun. For example, in the situation when our friend Jeremy asked for prayer for his mother, Mary, we prayed for Jeremy and Mary. We mentioned him and her, or they. Even if Jeremy is sitting right there with us, we wouldn't say, "you".

Here's why speaking in third person matters -- affirmative prayer is for the person praying, not the recipient of the prayer. We don't pray to make the other person feel better (though that often does happen). We pray to know the Truth in OUR OWN MIND, and therefore to impress that Truth into the Law of Cause and Effect. It doesn't matter if the person hears the prayer at all. The work is happening in our mind, which is one in the One Mind. We are, in effect, talking with the Indwelling God. Why would we talk to Jeremy in prayer when we can speak with the Spirit Consciousness at the center of our own being? We wouldn't.

**Loop Them into the Unification Step:** As we speak our prayer for someone else, the first step of prayer is unchanged. We recognize the Goodness of God in relation to that which is being claimed. When we get to the second step, Unification, things begin to expand. You'll start your Unification step exactly as you would normally, claiming your alignment with the Divine. However, before you complete this step, you'll also claim your prayer recipient's alignment with the Divine. This way, by the time you get to the Realization step, the logic is in place for a beautiful manifestation.

Your Unification step might sound like:

"I am made in the likeness and image of Infinite Spirit, containing the perfect pattern of Wholeness, Peace and Love. Everything that I am is made of this Spirit, and there is no aspect of the Divine that is missing in me. And as I know this Truth for myself, I know it for and about Jeremy. Jeremy is an expression of Divine Perfection, right here and right now. He is that same Peace, Love and Wholeness at the very center of his being. This is the Truth of his mother, Mary, as it is the Truth of all people."

**Speak our Word for the Person, by Name:** You might have noticed that the Realization steps I shared earlier in this chapter under the subheading "Speak in the Third Person" started a little bit differently than the one I shared in the chapter on Recognition. That's because it's important that we actually say that we are speaking our Word (the Word of God) for the specific person, by name. So, "I speak my word now for Amy, affirming that...." If our goal is to press firm belief into the Law of Universal Action, we need to be very, very clear what those beliefs are. I don't simply know the Truth of Abundance or Joy or whatever else Amy is seeking. I know they are the Truth OF AMY! So, I speak her name in the prayer, often and clearly.

**Thanksgiving:** In the Thanksgiving step, when we are praying for someone else, we give thanks for that person's good right here and right now. Again, we don't want this step to be abstract in any way. We are not thankful that God is Good. Well, I mean, we are...but that's not what this step is for. This step is for expressing gratitude about the fact that the things that have been prayed for are already true and real and present right now. No waiting, no striving, no seeking. That Good is already active in the life of the person we are praying for in this moment. Isn't that exciting?!

This is usually the step when I begin to cry. I am overwhelmed by the amazing feeling of absolute faith that washes through me, knowing that the wonderful things I have claimed for this person are real and true. It's powerful.

Your Thanksgiving Step might sound like this:
"I am so very grateful for Amy's overflowing Abundance, right here and right now. I give great thanks that the Word I have spoken for and about Amy is already true in the Heart and Mind of the One."

**Getting Over Fear:** Once we begin praying for other people, a very common thing can happen. We can have a crisis of confidence about the quality of our affirmative prayers.

Things I have heard from people in this stage include:
- My prayers are too short.
- My prayers are too long.
- My prayers don't flow like the Practitioners do at church.
- I don't know all the fancy language you guys use.
- I have to think about it, and no one else seems to need that.
- I'm afraid my prayer won't work and I'll let the person down.

It's essential that we remember that we are not doing the work in the prayer – God is. All we are responsible for is remembering the Truth for the person who we are praying for. It doesn't have to be flowery or poetic. It doesn't have to use any specific words or phrases. There isn't a magical correct length of prayer that works better than any other. Just use the five steps and it will work, I promise.

As you speak more prayers, as you practice and gain experience, it gets easier. You will find language that is particularly meaningful to you, and you'll use it. The five steps will become so natural that you won't even really think about them anymore. But all of this takes work. That's why I encourage (cajole? push? nag?) everyone to pray every single day, whether we need it or not. If we put the practice in now, we'll be able to focus on the prayer when the stuff really hits the fan.

# PRAYER PARTNER RELATIONSHIPS

The best way I know to gain significant prayer practice in a safe environment is to find a prayer partner. This is a person with whom you pray at agreed upon intervals. You might choose to meet weekly or monthly or according to some other schedule that makes sense to the two of you. You might prefer to meet in person, on the telephone or through a video call. What matters most is sticking to the agreement. After all, the only way out is through. The only way to get better at speaking affirmative prayers is to speak more affirmative prayers, and your prayer partner relationship will help you to do just that.

**Finding Resonance:** Of primary importance is to find someone that resonates with you. Spiritual people can sometimes struggle with this, because it can sit a little close to judgment or non-acceptance of all people exactly as they are. I really encourage you to let your concerns go in this situation. The truth is, if you don't resonate with your prayer partner, you'll find reasons not to pray with them. You'll "forget" appointments. You'll have trouble finding a time that works for you both. And, eventually, one or both of you will just give up. With the goal of regular shared prayer firmly in mind, look for someone who's energy you enjoy and who is looking for the same things you are in a prayer partner relationship.

**Scheduling:** This is such a mundane topic, but it can become a real issue in prayer partner relationships. It's really important that you and your PPP (potential prayer partner) are very clear and honest about how often you'd like to pray together and when you are available to pray. Partners with regular, scheduled appointments are much more likely to have a successful experience than those who decide to keep it loose and pray together when something comes up. Regular shared prayer builds the kind of relationship that can handle big crises when they come. If you haven't built that trust and intimacy, your prayer partner won't feel like a person you can share your troubles with. Be honest with yourself about what you are willing to commit to, and then commit.

**Choices of Prayer Styles:** There are three main prayer styles that prayer partners choose to share. Each one has highlights and challenges, and it really depends on your personal prayer partner relationship which style is best for you.

- **Live, You Pray, I Pray:** This is the most straightforward style of prayer partner sharing. It takes place live (in person, on the phone or via video chat). You tell me what you'd like prayer for, and I pray for you. Then I tell you what I'd like prayer for and you pray for me. Sometimes that's the entirety of the exchange – in that case, it only takes about 15 minutes for the call. More often, people have a bit of a chat about what's going on in their lives and kind of talk the issue out. This can help when someone knows what they'd like prayer about but haven't quite identified the qualities they are looking for. If this is the case, it is important to stick to whatever agreements you have in place regarding time, as this style of sharing can take 30 minutes or three hours, depending on how talkative you are. The highlight of this style of prayer is that it gives you the most practice speaking affirmative prayers. You also get to hear more complete affirmative prayers spoken and revel in the feeling of a prayer spoken just for you. The challenge can be time, if you are not careful to stick to your agreements. (Full disclosure: This is my favorite style, and I can't be unbiased about it. I'm also very chatty, as my four prayer partners will tell you, and they regularly have to remind me of our time commitment.)

- **Live, Round Robbin:** This type of prayer sharing starts out much the same as the "You Pray, I Pray" style, as it takes place like. In this style, you tell me what you'd like prayer for and I tell you what I'd like prayer for. Then I speak the Recognition Step and Unification Step for both of us, and the Recognition Step for you. You complete the prayer by speaking the second half of the Recognition Step for me, the Thanksgiving Step and the Releasing Step. (In a group of more than two, everyone in between the first and last partners speak just the Recognition Step.) The advantage of this prayer style is the beauty and power of a shared prayer. It also can shave a bit of time off your prayer appointment, as there is only one prayer spoken. The disadvantages are the same as the "You Pray, I Pray" style, as chattiness can get to us all. Additionally, you will get less practice, as you'll never speak an entire prayer yourself.

- **Off Site:** This final type of prayer sharing can show up in a number of ways. It can involve a live conversation where we name our prayer requests. It may be a quick exchange as you rush past each other in the hall on the way to a meeting. It might be an email or even a text message with your prayer needs. Then, each prayer partner speaks the requested prayer on their own at a convenient time. There are a lot of advantages to this style of prayer partnership if you are already very comfortable with affirmative prayer and don't need the practice praying in front of someone. It can be incredibly comforting to shoot off a text and know that your prayer partner has it under control. It's quick and dirty, takes virtually no time. The disadvantages are that you won't gain the experience of praying with others and hearing their prayers. This style of partnership doesn't offer nearly as much structure and support as the other styles. If you don't need that, maybe this is the style for you. I don't generally recommend it for people who are new to affirmative prayer.

**Questions to Ask a Potential Prayer Partner:** These questions will help you determine if you have found a fit. Take some time in thought and prayer around these questions. You should be prepared to answer them clearly and easily. Remember, there are no right or wrong answers to these questions. The goal is to find a true resonance and an excellent pairing that is mutually supportive. If someone doesn't want to pray with a beginner, better to know it now than when they get frustrated. Maybe you specifically want to pray with someone who is really solid in their prayer technique because you want to learn from them. If chatting makes you crazy, that should be on the table. If not being heard feels diminishing to you, that's important as well.

So, no judgment, here goes:

- What are you looking for in a prayer partner relationship?
- How often would you like to pray together?
- What days and times generally work for you for a prayer appointment?
- What style of prayer sharing do you prefer?
- Would you prefer to talk things out together, or are you happiest with a meeting that is only prayer requests and prayers?
- How much time are you willing to commit to our prayer appointments?
- How comfortable are you with speaking affirmative prayers in front of people?
- Are you willing to pray with someone who is still learning?

Praying for and with others is sure to deepen and enrich your affirmative prayer experience. My prayer partners have a huge part of my spiritual growth (and my sanity!) for the past decade. My wish for each of you is that you find the perfect powerful, loving prayer partner for you.

# PRAYING FOR GROUPS

There are a lot of opportunities to utilize affirmative prayer in the world, and one of them is praying for groups. It might be an opening or closing prayer at an event. It might be a blessing over a meal. It might be a prayer to resolve a conflict during a meeting or to invoke a desired quality, like Peace or Love. Regardless of the situation, we can be a source of positivity and light through our prayer. We just need to make sure that we are aligned with the reason we were invited to pray, for the highest good of all.

Determining the Intention and Purpose: Before the prayer, or even before the event if possible, talk with the person who has invited you to pray. Finding out the following things before the prayer will help you speak a prayer that is both affirmative and specialized to meet the needs of the group:

- What is their intention with this prayer? Are we kicking off an event? Are we blessing the food before a feast? Are we calling forth world peace? We need to know.

- Do they want a full 5-step affirmative prayer or would they prefer a short blessing? (Do they even know what a 5-step affirmative prayer is? Lots of people don't.)

- What qualities of Spirit would they like to affirm for this event/meeting/group?

- Is this a multi-faith group, and is there any language we should be sensitive to?

- What, if anything, are they concerned about?

Once you have a sense of the nature of the event and the kind of prayer they are looking for, it's easy to speak the perfect 5-step affirmative prayer for this particular group. You just identify the God Qualities desired and follow the formula we've learned in this book.

I hear you, though. You're saying, "But what if they say they want a short blessing. Are there rules for short blessings? What are invocations and benedictions? You haven't covered any of this! I'm freaking out!!"

Breathe, dear reader. Short blessings are easy and sweet. Each kind of short blessing has a few things that must be included, but we have a great deal of freedom with structure in this form of prayer. They tend to be quick (hence the "short" in short blessings) and fairly simple.

**Invocations:** Also known as opening blessings, opening prayers or "praying us in," an invocation is designed to invoke (or acknowledge) the presence of Spirit. Usually placed at the very beginning of a meeting or gathering, we bless the coming events. We affirm any desired qualities. We express gratitude for all that is unfolding, and end the prayer with "Amen" or "And so it is."

You will notice that I've said nothing about steps. You don't need to worry about that here. You'll also notice that we didn't release the Word into the Law. That's because we're not seeking to manifest anything. We are simply celebrating the Presence of the Divine and calling it Good.

**Benedictions:** Also known as closing blessings, closing prayers or "praying us out," a benediction is spoken to express gratitude for everything that has transpired. We affirm the ongoing expression of any desired qualities and bless each person safely on their way. Once again, we end the prayer with "Amen" or "And so it is." Once again, there is no need to follow steps or to release anything into the Law. We are just thankful for the wonderful things that happened here.

**Blessing of the Meal:** Also known as "saying grace," this sweet and simple blessing is spoken before we eat. It is traditional to express gratitude for the nutritious food and for the loving hands that prepared it. Many people choose to share a word of thanks for all of the Abundance and Good of Spirit. Finally, we close with "Amen" or "And so it is."

While prayer opportunities for groups are more likely to be for multi-faith crowds than most other kinds of prayers, there is no need to worry. As long as your prayer invites everyone in by using inclusive language and stays positive and affirmative, your prayer can be a powerful gift to the group.

## Beverley's Prayer Experience

**Affirmative Prayer changes everything.**

**Using the power of my words to change my experience is indeed a life-changing concept. Not only does Affirmative Prayer change how the world responds to me, it changes how I see the world. It guides me to state, claim and accept that which is already mine in the Mind of God. It inspires me, but what brings me to awe is its simplicity.**

**Say it. Claim it. Experience it.**

# AFFIRMATIVE PRAYER LIBRARY

There are few things I enjoy more than writing an affirmative prayer, but that has not always been the case. When I first started learning about 5-step prayers, I was overwhelmed and confused. I was frustrated when I couldn't think of the exact right word or turn of phrase, and it felt like I would never get it right. If you are feeling this way, take a breath. YOU ARE NORMAL. It's completely reasonable to feel like you're not getting it. The trick is to keep going anyway, which is where this chapter comes in.

    The prayers in this library are written for you to read, play with, customize, steal from and use in any way you find helpful. I wrote them in the first person, so they will read as if you write them for yourself. You can utilize them as is, or (even better), you can change the words to more perfectly fit your situation. Consider them a jumping-off point, a springboard into writing your own fully custom affirmative prayers. I included the name of each step here to help you learn the 5-Step process, but you don't need to read them aloud when you say the prayer.

    You will notice that each step is written differently for each of the prayers. This is intentional, to give you many examples of ways to start a Recognition step or a Unification step. Building your own inner vocabulary for prayer takes time, but this is a little shortcut for you. Take note of the phrases that really work for you and try using them when you write your own prayers. Similarly, pay attention to the phrases and names of God that get your hackles up, and just don't use them in the future. Having lots of examples will make this process quicker and easier for you than it was for me. You're welcome.

Remember, if you use this prayer library to create prayers for other people, you'll need to modify them into the third person (speaking of "them" or by name). Refer back to the section "Praying for Someone Else" for pointers on how to choose the best wording for prayers for others. It's actually good practice, as it will help you understand more fully the structural prayer differences when praying for someone else. Again, your welcome. (I do so love assigning homework!)

If you are serious about reading and writing affirmative prayers every day, you'll be speeding through this process in no time. I'm thrilled for you, knowing that mastering the art of affirmative prayer will revolutionize your life. I can't wait to see what you do next!

# PRAYER FOR HEALTH

(Recognition) There is one Power, one Spirit, one Creator Source of all of Life. This One is Good. It is Health and Wholeness, Energy and Vitality, Joy and Ease. It is the Power that put the very stars in motion. And this One is expressing perfectly in, through and as all of Life. Every person, everything and every situation is an expression of this One that we call God. It is everywhere present, right here and right now.

(Unification) I recognize that I am a divine emanation of this One. I am an expression of God, made whole, perfect and complete, just as I am. Because this is true, everything I claim for God, I must recognize in myself. I am Health and Wholeness, Energy and Vitality, Joy and Ease. I am divinely guided to perfect right action by the still small voice at the center of myself.

(Realization) And so, knowing this truth, I speak my Word for my perfect, Divine health. The wholeness that I already am is activated, called forth to reveal the glory of God in my glowing, radiant health. Every cell, every tissue, every organ, every system operates perfectly and in harmony with my whole body. I overflow with energy, vitally alive in every way. Any and all thoughts, ideas or habits of illness, pain or injury are just gone, back to the nothingness from which they came. They have no power here. Nothing can keep me from my Divine birthright, which is perfect health.

(Thanksgiving) I am so thankful for the Truth of this Word, knowing that it is already manifesting powerfully in my life.

(Release) And so I release this Word into the action of Universal Law, which has already said yes. I let it go. And so it is.

# PRAYER TO PREPARE FOR SURGERY

(Recognition) It is so good to take this time to turn my attention to the Source of All That Is, the One Power and Presence of the Divine. It is all that there is, at the heart of every being, making up the Universe out of Its own Beingness. This One is Perfect Intelligence, knowing and understanding all. It is Wisdom and Kindness, Grace and Wholeness. It is the One Mind, in which rests all knowledge, all discernment, all healing.

(Unification) As a part of All That Is, I must recognize that I am one with The One, made in Its likeness and having access to Its Divine qualities. My mind is one with the One Mind, my heart is one with the One Heart. So, I am Intelligence and Wisdom, Kindness and Grace. I am a seat of Wholeness and healing, right here and right now. And as I know this truth for myself, I know it for every person who in any way affects my health care. I know that Divine Intelligence and Perfect Wisdom are at work within every doctor, surgeon, nurse and aide that assists on my case. I know Kindness and Grace to be in the hearts of all who visit me, who pray for me, who think kindly of me during my healing process.

(Realization) And so, I speak my Word for my perfect health, knowing that The One is working mightily through each of us to perform a wondrous miracle of healing. Intelligence and Wisdom are revealed as excellent decision-making and brilliant performances by every doctor on my case. Kindness and Grace are revealed through warm and thoughtful care. Ease and Wholeness are revealed through a perfect unfoldment of my surgery and recovery, demonstrating the Divine pattern of health in every way. I let fall away from me any and every fear or doubt, for they are not the truth and they have no power. Instead, I trust deeply that God is at work in my life and in my body, supporting me every step of the way. I am loved and I am well.

(Thanksgiving) I am grateful, grateful, grateful for the perfect healing that is mine right now. I am grateful for my doctors, my nurses, my family and my friends who have supported me beautifully. I am grateful to know that I am well.

(Release) And so I let it go, imprinting my intention on the Law of Creative Mind, and trusting that my perfect healing is brought forth into manifest form. I let God do God's job. I know that it is done. And so it is.

# PRAYER FOR FAITH AND SURRENDER

(Recognition) There is one Life. This Life is God's Life. This Life is perfect, a beautiful unfoldment of all things Good, expressing as everything that is. It is that still small voice of guidance that always leads to the highest and best. It is Love and Grace, Support and Supply. It is deep Peace, full faith and powerful surrender.

(Unification) What I know for myself is that God's perfect Life is my life now. I can never be separate from It, for It is the building blocks of everything that I am. The Truth of me is Peace and Grace and Perfect Love. I am built for surrender into faith.

(Realization) And so I speak my Word for a profound sense of absolute calm and ease in every area of my life. I let go of needing to know the answers, as I am Divinely guided in every moment to perfect right action and right outcome. I easily and effortlessly surrender every question, every relationship and every feeling into the Grace of Sweet Spirit, trusting completely that I am supported and supplied in all things. I lean into my faith, feeling The Beloved in all that I experience. My affairs are run by the Most High, and I am truly blessed.

(Thanksgiving) I give grateful, grateful thanks for this sense of faith, surrender and powerful trust. I am thankful for the beautiful way Spirit graces all of life.

(Release) I release this prayer into the perfect activity of the Law of Mind with a complete sense of trust that it is done now. It is good. And so it is.

# PRAYER FOR PEACE OF MIND

(Recognition) There is one Universal Life that makes Itself known in individualized form as each individual person and thing. This One Life is the same Energy that allows the sun to shine and the fields to grow, naturally and effortlessly bringing forth more goodness into every moment. It guides and guards all with Love and Grace, ensuring that all is well, no matter what.

(Unification) Knowing that this One Life exists everywhere, I affirm my oneness with It and claim Its qualities as present within me. The Love of the Divine pours through me. The Grace of the Divine washes over me. The same Divine Energy that creates and sustains all of nature is within me now and in every moment. I am safe and secure, guarded and guided in every way by the indwelling Spirit. All is well with me, always.

(Realization) And so I speak my Word for a profound sense of absolute Peace in every moment. I see the things that are going on in the world, and yet I see beyond them to the Divine Truth that everything and everyone is being cared for by The Beloved One. I am guided in every action, guarded from any harm; thus, I am completely safe. My world is completely safe, run by the perfect, all-knowing Spirit that is ever-present. Every part of my being relaxing into the knowingness that God has got this, and all is truly well.

(Thanksgiving) I am so grateful for this amazing Truth of Peace in every area of my life. I breathe easy and give thanks for all the good in my life now.

(Release) I release this prayer into the perfect activity of the Law of Mind with a complete sense of trust that it is done now. It is good. And so it is.

# PRAYER FOR CLARITY

(Recognition) God is all there is. There is nothing that stands against It, and there is nothing else to be. It is the Alpha and the Omega, omnipresent and omnipotent. It is literally everything, as everything and everyone are made out of Its substance. As the One Mind, It contains all knowledge, every idea and infinite possibilities. It is Clarity and Wisdom, Divine Intelligence and perfect Guidance.

(Unification) My mind is of the One Mind, and I have access to all that It contains, because I am one with my Creator. At the center of my being is already encoded Wisdom, Clarity and Divine Intelligence. I am forever guided, forever led by the Indwelling Spirit.

(Realization) And so I speak my Word for absolute Clarity in my life. I am present to the whisper of Divine Guidance, leading me always to perfect right action and ideal outcome. My next step is made clear before me, and the resources I need to take that step are always provided by The One. Graceful solutions appear before me with Ease. I know what to do and when to do it for the highest and best outcome of all, and every bit of it is easy because it has always been the Truth.

(Thanksgiving) How grateful I am to live in the knowingness that I am Divinely guided and have perfect clarity in my life. I am so thankful that Life is Good!

(Release) With a gracious heart, I release this prayer into the Law, knowing it is done. I trust it. I let it be. And so it is.

# PRAYER FOR FOCUS

(Recognition) I turn within, to the space where Truth resides, and there I recognize the Power and the Presence of the Almighty, the One Mind, the All Knowing. This One, with laser focus and absolute Clarity, created all of life and imbued Its creation with Its very Essence. There is nowhere God is not, and no part of It is missing in anyone or anything. It is powerful intention and Divine Intelligence, making Itself known in all things.

(Unification) This is what I know for myself: I am created by that same Almighty Power. It has imprinted Itself on my heart, building me out of Its own stuff and substance, in Its likeness and image. Every aspect of this One is a part of me, built into my very DNA by my Creator. The focus and intention of the Divine is right here within me. The Clarity and Intelligence of God is always mine to claim and express.

(Realization) And so, I speak my Word, affirming that I am perfect focus in all of my affairs. I complete each task before me easily, completely free from distraction or confusion. I see each step clearly, and take action on each with Ease. Divine Intelligence operates through me as a perfect Knowingness about what to do and when to do it, lining every element up beautifully with ideal timing and magnificent outcome. Nothing has the power to pull my attention or my intention away from my focused choices. Nothing can keep me from my good.

(Thanksgiving) Gratitude wells up from the core of me, flowing forth with thanks and praise. I am so grateful for the focus in my life.

(Release) I let it go, releasing it into the Law of Cause and Effect, trusting that it is done. I let it be. And so it is.

# PRAYER FOR CREATIVITY

(Recognition) There is an Infinite Presence, an omnipotent Intelligence, that is the organizing Principle of All of Life. This One that we call Spirit is in all, of all, as all, expressing as the powerful and beautiful unfoldment of absolute Perfection. It is forever and ever expanding, as It creates more Life out of Itself. It is the very Essence of Creativity.

(Unification) As a creation of this One, I am made of that which It is. As such, I am creative in my nature. There is no part of me that is separate from Spirit, and no aspect of Spirit which is missing in me. Creativity, expression, the calling forth of more, is built into my beingness by That Which Made Me. I can be nothing less, for nothing made of God can be lessened.

(Realization) And I speak my Word right here and right now, claiming my own profound creativity. The Divine Creative Truth of my nature shows up as a connection to my own inner Intelligence and Wisdom, pouring forth wonderful and innovative ideas. It shows up as the revelation of my expression and expansion as I develop those ideas. And it shows up as the activation of my order, discipline and balance as I act upon those ideas. I manifest my Divine ideas powerfully in the manifest realm of the physical world.

(Thanksgiving) I am grateful, grateful, grateful to recognize my powerful creative nature, knowing that my ideas are already in the Mind of God, and are heading to manifestation right now.

(Release) With complete trust and faith, I release this spiritual mind treatment into the Law of Cause and Effect. I know that it is done unto me as I believe, so I know that it is done. And so it is.

# PRAYER FOR JOY

(Recognition) All of life is surrounded by and connected by an Infinite Energy that is pure Source. It is called God by some, Divine Mind by others, but It is the only thing there truly is. This Spirit is the very fount of Joy, of the bubbling forth of the Goodness of Life, every flowing forth. It is Wholeness and pure Love in Its most natural form.

(Unification) Source Energy is the Truth of who I am, as I am literally made of It and express It in all that I am. I am an emanation of Divine Joy, shining forth the pure Goodness of my nature. Made in the likeness and image of my Creator, there is nothing else for me to be but It's Love, Wholeness and Joy.

(Realization) And so I speak my Word right here and right now, recognizing and affirming that I am absolute Joy. The spiritual quality of Joy that has been built into the perfect pattern of my beingness is activated powerfully, shining forth and calling into my life a sweet positivity, ringing laughter and deep friendship. I simply allow it to rise to the surface, as my Joy has always been the Truth.

(Thanksgiving) My grateful heart wells up to overflowing for the wonder of my Joyful life, right here and right now. I'm so thankful to know that the Word I have spoken is already done.

(Release) I Joyfully release this prayer into the Law, knowing that it is already rushing into manifestation in my life. I let it go, knowing that the entire Universe is conspiring for my good. And so it is.

# PRAYER TO RELEASE OVERWHELM

(Recognition) I take a deep breath and dive in, immersing myself in the Power and Presence of the All Good. This One Power that created all things in perfect balance and wisdom is ever present and contains every possibility. It is Divine right timing and flowing abundance of all that could ever be needed. It is Ease and Grace, Calm and Peace. It is the perfect and beautiful unfoldment of Life for the highest and best of all.

(Unification) Surrounded by this Oneness, I affirm that I am a part of It, as It has created me out of Itself. Within me is the Divine patterning of Grace and Peace, Ease and Calm. My nature is Abundance, and I am always guided to right action and right timing. Everything I could ever want is accessible at the center of myself.

(Realization) And so, I speak this Word for my own Freedom as I release this sense of overwhelm from my body, from my mind and from my heart. I powerfully activate the Peace and Calm that are the Truth of my nature, breathing deeply and feeling God's Grace pour over me. It melts away any fear, any stress, any sense of being behind or overworked. I recognize that Divine timing is always at work in my life, and I open to the guidance that is always leading me closer to the Indwelling Source. I am always at the right place, doing the perfect thing at the ideal moment, and everything is being handled by the One that created me. All is well, right here and right now, and I am at Peace.

(Thanksgiving) I give my thanks for the powerful blessings of this truth in my life now.

(Release) I release my Word into the Law of Creative Mind with absolute trust and complete peace. I call it good and very good. And so it is.

# PRAYER FOR ACCEPTANCE AND TOLERANCE

(Recognition) Expressing in and through and as All of Life is One Pure Love that I call Spirit. In Spirit, all is exactly as it should be, unfolding beautifully and perfectly according to the Law of Life. It is Whole and complete, exactly as It is and in every incarnation. It is the Love and Wisdom that drives acceptance and tolerance of all beings and all situations.

(Unification) As I am made of pure Spirit, I express Its Love and Wisdom with my entire being. Whole and complete exactly as I am, it is my natural state to be Spirit in form.

(Realization) And so I speak my Word for myself, affirming that the Love and Wisdom that I am rise up within me and shine more brightly than ever before. I am guided and led by Indwelling Spirit to live in acceptance and tolerance of everyone I meet, including those who think and believe differently than I do. I recognize that all beings are expressions of Divine Perfection, and so I know that each person is doing the very best they can in this perfect now moment. I bless each beloved soul, and know that Love and Wisdom are active in each of their hearts. I act from a place of kindness and Love, trusting that all is well right here and right now.

(Thanksgiving) I am deeply thankful for the Love and Wisdom in my life now. I'm grateful for my accepting and tolerant nature.

(Release) I release this Word into the Law, thankful that my acceptance and tolerance are already the Truth right now. I let it be, trusting that it is so. And so it is.

# PRAYER FOR BLESSING A NEW BABY

(Recognition) In the Beauty and Perfection of God there is a profound Joy, bubbling up as Life Itself. It is present in every being, in all that has every been and all that ever will be, as it is the nature of the Divine. Expressing in and through and as all things, the Perfection of God is all there is.

(Unification) I am a walking, talking manifestation of that Divine Perfection, as I am an expression of the One God. Joy and Beauty are my Truth, as I am made in complete Wholeness. Knowing this Truth for myself, I recognize it to be the Truth of all beings everywhere. Most especially, I see it as the Truth of this Beloved New Baby.

(Realization) And so I speak my Word of blessing for this precious new life, affirming that (s)he is made in the likeness and image of absolute Perfection. Beauty and Wholeness is her Truth. Joy flows forth from within her and blesses all in her presence. She is Wholeness in mind, body and spirit, more than enough exactly as she is. The Love of God surrounds her. The Grace of God protects her. The Givingness of God supplies all she ever will need.

(Thanksgiving) My heart sings in joy and gratitude for the blessings of this little one, Whole, Joy-filled and Perfect right here and right now.

(Release) I release this Word into the Universal Law of Truth, confident that it is done as I have spoken. And so it is.

# PRAYER FOR WISDOM FOR OUR WORLD LEADERS

(Recognition) And so I turn within to the very center of myself, to the place where I know that I know that I know that there is only One – One Truth, One Power, One Grace, One Glory, One Perfect Creator-Source of All of Life. What I know is that this One Mind is All-Powerful. It contains all Knowledge and all Wisdom. It is simply the Truth. This One is goodness made manifest. It is pouring forth Divine Intelligence. It is perfect Order, leading to Divine Right Action in every moment, all the time, no matter what. This One that I call God is Peace and Love for everyone and everything. It is that which calls forth the perfect unfoldment for the highest and best of this life and all life.

(Unification) What I know for myself is that I am that which It is. I am an emanation of Divine Perfection, made in the likeness and image of my Creator. So, I am that Wisdom. I am that Divine Intelligence, that Knowingness beyond knowingness. The very core of my being is suffused with the Presence and Power of The Beloved, with the Peace and Grace of God Itself. And because I know this Truth for myself, I know that it is the truth of all people, for each and every one is made in the likeness and image of the same All-Knowing, All-Powerful Divine Presence. We are, every one of us, overflowing with perfect Wisdom and Divine Order. The leaders of our world, the political leaders and religious leaders and those who have risen to the top of the populace to become leaders of the people, each and every one of these leaders is suffused with the same Wisdom, the same Grace, the same Glory. They are each guided by an Indwelling Voice of Peace, of Compassion, of Grace and understanding.

(Realization) And so, knowing the Truth about each leader in our world, I speak my Word for them now, recognizing that the Wisdom that they already are at the very center of their beings, imprinted in their very DNA, that this Wisdom is activated right here, right now. This Wisdom is brought forth to reveal more of the Goodness and Glory that is God. I recognize and know that this Wisdom guides each and every leader to make decisions for the very highest and best of ALL of their people, and to recognize that every citizen of the world deserves a life of Freedom, equality, Abundance and safety. I know perfect Balance in the leadership of our world, allowing for a deep and abiding Peace between all nations, all ethnic groups and all religions. I affirm that the voice speaking in the heart of every leader is one of Love – pure, Divine, accepting Love.

(Thanksgiving) And I am so thankful to know that this is already so in the heart of God, in the center of Divine Truth. So thankful to know that this simply must come forth into manifest form because that's the way the Universe works.

(Release) I release this Word into the action of Universal Law, trusting completely that it is done. I let it be. And so it is.

# PRAYER FOR FINANCIAL ABUNDANCE

(Recognition) How good it is to rest in the Truth that Sweet Spirit is all there is. That there is One Truth, One Presence, One Source of All-That-Is. And this One is expressing in, through and as all of Creation. It is deep Love and abiding Peace. It is Prosperity overflowing and never-ending Abundance. It is the ever-givingness of Life. It is all Good.

(Unification) I recognize that I am an expression of this One, unique and yet in complete unity with All-That-Is. I am made up of God-stuff, Divine in my nature. All that I do, all that I am, is Divinity expressing. And as such, I am all that I claim for God -- I am Love and Peace. I am Prosperity at the very core of my being. I am that flowing Abundance, and am constantly experiencing the givingness of Life. I am made in the image of Divine perfection, just exactly as I am. Ease and Grace is the Truth of who I am.

(Realization) And from this deep understanding of the Truth of my life, I speak my Word for now for my flowing Abundance. I recognize the Divine quality of Prosperity showing up in my life as more than enough money to easily meet all my needs and more to share. I see my every bill and debt paid in full, right here, right now. I know that the entire Universe is conspiring for my good, filling my bank account and settling all of my financial responsibilities with Ease and Grace. Any and all thoughts or beliefs in lack, poverty or fear are banished, back into the nothingness from whence they came. I claim for myself only Abundance and Prosperity from this day forth.

(Thanksgiving) I am so thankful to know that the Word I speak is already true in the Mind of God, so it must come forth into the manifest world. I am grateful beyond grateful to know it is so.

(Release) And so I release this Word into the Law that is the Creative Medium, knowing it is already done. I let God do God's work. And so it is.

# PRAYER FOR THE PERFECT JOB

(Recognition) Such a gift it is to turn within and remember the truth, which simply is the One Perfect Power and Presence that is the Divine. This one Perfect Presence has made Itself known through every man, every woman, every child, every situation and every circumstance; beautifully and powerfully unfolding for the highest and best of all life. It is Abundance and Prosperity pouring forth. It is competence and confidence, Intelligence and productivity. It is Creativity in its truest sense, continually bringing Itself into manifest form as all that is. It is Ease and Grace, Flow and Joy, Guidance and Goodness.

(Unification) And what I know is this: That is what I am. I am made of that perfect God-stuff. Everything that I am, everything that I do, everything that I say, everything that I think flows from that core of Divine Truth. I am productivity and competence. I am Divine Wisdom and Intelligence in every area of my life. I am Abundance and Prosperity pouring forth, guided in Ease and Grace. I am the place where God shows up.

(Realization) And so I speak my Word for my life, recognizing that this profound Divine Truth shows up for me as the perfect job for me right here, right now. The competence, confidence and Divine Wisdom that I am show up as powerful interviews, where my magnificence shines clearly, allowing all to see me in my highest light and showing the Truth of who I am at my very best. The Prosperity and Abundance that I am calls forth a job that pays more than enough to meet my needs. I am Divinely guided to a job that fits my personal skills beautifully; a job that deeply satisfies me by powerfully inspiring my passion, my creativity and my dedication. And I recognize that every step of the way is easy and grace-filled and good. What I know is that which I seek is seeking me, because that's how the Universe works. My new employer has asked for everything that I am, and I am a gift to my new company.

(Thanksgiving) I am so thankful to know beyond a shadow of a doubt that this Word I speak is true, and that I speak it with the spiritual authority of God Itself because that's the truth of who I am – an emanation of powerful Divine Goodness.

(Release) And so I release this Word, knowing that it is acted upon powerfully by the Law, showing up in manifest form in ways that amaze and delight me. It is good. It is very good. And so it is.

# PRAYER FOR A SUCCESSFUL MEETING

(Recognition) All of Life is One. It is an Infinite Unity, a perfect Wholeness, containing endless variation within a beautiful Oneness. And this Divine One is Harmony and Joy, Peace and Willingness. In the One Mind is every answer, every option, every potentiality for every situation that ever has been or ever will be. It is in every person, expressing as every relationship and through every unfoldment. There is nothing outside of this Truth, and nothing else for anyone or anything to be. There is only One.

(Unification) As a part of this One, I know that every solution is available to me. That I am already the Harmony and Joy of God right now. That Its Peace and Willingness shine in my heart. That I am Divinely guided in what to do, what to say, how to be in every situation. And I recognize this same truth for everyone I will ever meet, most especially those who will participate in this meeting. They are each one in the One, guided and uplifted by the Indwelling Spirit.

(Realization) And so this is what I know for our meeting today. I claim and declare that everything that needs to be known comes up easily and effortlessly. I know that each member of the group is guided to know what is important and what can fall away, to listen with an open heart and mind to all sides, and to make decisions that are for the highest and best of all involved. I trust that Intelligence and Wisdom are revealed powerfully through each of us, so that a mighty work can be done. I know that the Divine oversees a powerful and successful meeting for us all.

(Thanksgiving) All glory goes to God, as It makes known what has always been so. I am thankful to know that the perfect outcome of this meeting is already done in the Mind of God, so it is already coming forth into the physical world now. It is done.

(Release) I release this Word into Universal Law with complete trust. I let it be. And so it is.

# PRAYER TO SELL A HOUSE

(Recognition) God, the Divine, Perfect Beloved One is all that there is. Whole, perfect and complete in Its essence, It contains all that ever has been and ever will be. It is everything fitting into exactly the right spaces through Divine Guidance, Ease and Flow. This One Perfect Energy made every single thing that there is out of Itself, so that everything fits the Divine Patterning of absolute Grace. It is Abundance and Prosperity. It is Harmony and Divine Timing. It is everything Good, right here and right now.

(Unification) And what I know about my life is that that is the Truth of who I am. That I am Divine Perfection making Itself known in manifest form as this version of God, this emanation of Divine Goodness, made in Its likeness and image. I am imbued with everything that my Creator is, at the very center of my being. That same Abundance, that same Divine Timing, that Ease and Grace and Flow is the Truth of who I am. And as I know this to be my Truth, I know it also to be the Truth of every person selling a house, every Realtor, every Loan Officer, every single person at every step of the home selling path. Each is guided and led by the Indwelling One.

(Realization) And so this is the word I speak today. The right person to buy my house is seeking it right now. The entire Universe is conspiring to bring together the perfect individuals to sell a home and to buy a home, so that everyone gets exactly what they need for their highest benefit. And all along, every step of the way is falling into place. Loans are being secured easily and effortlessly. Inspections are being passes. Little glitches are cleaned up with Ease and Harmony. This house sells right now, closes on time and everything is perfect!

(Thanksgiving) I'm thankful to know this Truth for everybody involved in this process! I'm grateful for my sold house, and I'm grateful for the new buyer's successful home purchase, right here and right now! It is so Good!

(Release) And knowing it is already done, I release this Word into Universal Law and impress my belief into that Creative Medium. I let it go and celebrate! And so it is.

# PRAYER FOR A NEW ROMANTIC PARTNER

(Recognition) And so I drop down into the center of myself, into that place where all I see and all I know is the absolute Perfection that is God's Grace. The Wholeness and the Beauty, containing everything, making all of Life out of Itself so that every person, every place, everything is Divine in its own nature. God is pure, unconditional Love. This One that I call Sweet Spirit is Kindness and Compassion. It is humor and Integrity. It is All Things Good.

(Unification) And what I know is that God is literally what I am made of. I am an expression of the Divine, brought forth by my Creator just as I am – whole, perfect and complete. There is no part of me that is separate from God and no Divine quality that is not written on my heart. I am that Love and that Kindness, that deep Compassion and Integrity. I am humor and passion and Joy. And just as I know this is true of my life, I know that it is true of everyone I meet.

(Realization) And knowing this truth, I speak my Word claiming and affirming that I have a committed, loving romantic relationship right here and right now. I am an expression of Divine Love and Perfection, which manifests as deep Love reflecting back to me. I am Divinely guided to perfect right action in every area of my life, in every relationship, and everything is working out for my highest and best. The ideal people are attracted to my True Nature, bringing me a healthy and loving relationship with one who demonstrates integrity, kindness, compassion and humor. Any and all thoughts, ideas or beliefs about loneliness are gone, back to the nothingness from which they came. Pain has no power, it is not real. Only God is real, and God is deep, abiding love.

(Thanksgiving) I am so thankful to know this Word is already so in the Mind of God and is rushing into my physical life right now.

(Release)  And so I release this Word into the Law that is the Creative Medium, trusting that it is done.  And so it is.

# PRAYER FOR A HEALED RELATIONSHIP

(Recognition) I recognize the Presence everywhere of a wondrous, unconditional Love. This Love includes all, accepts all and embraces all that is. I know this Love as the God of My Understanding, the Infinite Force of Good in this world. There is nowhere this Love is not, and no one is excluded from It. I recognize this Love as the only Power that is.

(Unification) As an emanation of this Love, made in Its likeness and image, I recognize that this same Love lives in me. There is nothing for me to be, other than an expression of the One that brought me forth. I am the Good of God, the acceptance of God and the perfect Love of God. And as I know this to be my Truth, I know it to be the Truth of all people, including and especially (*your beloved person*). I affirm that (s)he is the Love of the Divine.

(Realization) And so I speak my Word for the relationship between (your beloved person) and me. I affirm that the Love that we each are is activated powerfully right here and right now by Divine Grace, melting away any and all hurt feelings, bad memories and unkind interactions. I call upon the qualities of compassion and forgiveness in each one of us to make themselves known as a willingness to see the Divine Truth of one another. We are each soothed and comforted in Sweet Spirit as we look anew upon our beloved one, experiencing a deep healing and a fresh beginning in Love. In God, all things are made new.

(Thanksgiving) Giving grateful praise for the Love in my life, I celebrate this healed relationship. I am so thankful for the Truth of this Word now.

(Release) And so I let it go, releasing my Word into the perfect action of the Law of Cause and Effect. I trust that God is handling it all. And so it is.

# PRAYER FOR FORGIVENESS

(Recognition) I turn my attention and my awareness to the only thing that is True – the
never-ending and overflowing Perfection and Grace of Sweet Spirit, in and through all of Life. It is the All Good, the Mother Father God, the Perfect Presence. It is the beautiful unfoldment of Goodness in all things, for the highest and best of all. It is the still small voice of Divine guidance and discernment, and the sweet release of everything that no longer serves.

(Unification) And as I am made up of the Goodness That Created Me, that Truth is present in my being, too. The still small voice speaks in the depths of my soul, leading me and guiding me. I am the Infinite Capacity for Perfection and Grace, for Beauty and release, for endless Love. There is no part of God that is absent in me, no place in me that is anything other than the Divine.

(Realization) And so I speak this Word of Truth about my life, affirming that the Love and Grace that is already present within me is more deeply revealed as a falling-away of everything that is ready to be released. I do not claim that what happened was acceptable. And yet, I realize that this grudge I carry hurts no one but myself. And so, I forgive. I access the powerful discernment within myself to put down that rock of hurt and anger and shame. I release it from my mind, from my body, from my soul, for it was never mine to carry. I refuse to allow the poison of that experience to taint even one more day of my life. I forgive, allowing the Grace of God to work within me, cleansing my heart and making me new. I release my transgressor from the bondage of my judgment, and I release myself from the responsibility of punishment. I let Spirit do Its job of running the Universe, and rise up with the lightness and Freedom of sweet release. I trust that all is well, right here and right now.

(Thanksgiving) And my heart overflows with gratitude for the Beauty of it all. I am thankful for the lightness I feel in my heart right now. I am grateful, knowing that this prayer is already the Truth in the Mind of God, and that Spirit is at work in me right now bringing it into physical reality. I give some mighty thanks that I am able to forgive.

(Release) So I release this prayer, trusting completely that it is done. The Law of Cause and Effect accepts this prayer into Its Divine Mechanism, amplifying my intention and bringing it forth into magnificent manifestation. It is done. And so it is.

# PRAYER TO RELEASE THE PAST

(Recognition) All is well at the heart of Divine Goodness, the One and Only God, which is all there is. Within this One is contained every solution, every answer, ever resolution and every potentiality. It is the original home of Love and Grace, of renewal and healing, of strength and transformation. This One washes all things clean, wiping away all that no longer fits and providing paths to the new. In It, there is no danger, no lack, no pain. It is the only Truth.

(Unification) I know that I am of this One, this Divine Goodness. It made me, just as It made all of life, and it filled me with Its own qualities of Love and Grace. I have access to Divine renewal and healing in every moment. At the center of my own being is the Strength and Wisdom to affect powerful transformation.

(Realization) And this is what I know for my life now. I affirm that right now, right at this very moment, Divine Love is the Truth of my entire being. From that place of perfect Love, I allow Grace to heal every wound from my past. All of my sharp edges are smoothed, and all hardness of my heart is softened. I allow to fall away from me now any attachment to the story of my past, any and all beliefs that I am limited in any way by my history. I am transformed, Free from every excuse, every stuck-ness, every blockage. I am complete pure Freedom, right here and right now, open to an entirely new way of living and loving. My past is gone, and I am blossoming in the Light of the One.

(Thanksgiving) I am beyond thankful for the lightness, the Freedom, that I feel right now. My past is gone, and I am transformed. It is so good!

(Release) So I release this prayer into the Law of Mind, with complete faith that it has always been the truth. I let it go. And so it is.

# PRAYER FOR GRIEF

(Recognition) Here's what I know for sure – there is a Power greater than me in the Universe. It is Divine in Its nature, all-knowing and ever-present. It created the moon and the stars and set the worlds into motion. It is eternal and unchanging, and It is only Good. This Power I call God Almighty, the Divine Mind. It expresses as all of life, in all forms, in all experiences.

(Unification) And what I know for myself is that I am one with this Power. Its changeless and eternal Energy lives in every cell of my being, breathing me to life. Its Goodness and Its Grace is written in my DNA. Because I am of It, my soul is immortal and I am forever filled with the Perfect Love and Wholeness of the Divine. As it's true for me, it is true of all people, as we are all one with the One who created us. It's absolutely the Truth of my beloved, who has transitioned into Spirit.

(Realization) In this absolute knowingness, I speak my Word knowing that the Grace of God pours down over me, soothing and comforting me in my grief. It reminds me of the Truth, that my beloved is safe and secure in the pure Love of the Divine and that (s)he is well, right here and right now. Sweet Spirit strengthens me as I adjust to this new life, filling me with hope and carrying me through all I must do. I am never alone, for the One is always within me.

(Thanksgiving) I am beyond thankful for this comfort, for the ever-presence of this Grace.

(Release) I release this Word into Universal Law, knowing that It is always acting on the impress of my thoughts. I let it be. And so it is.

# PRAYER OF GRATITUDE

(Recognition) I recognize God as the Source and Supply of all that is: all life, all form, all manifestation. This One that I call The Beloved is the Wellspring of all things Good, pouring forth Love and Grace, Peace and Beauty through Its own Infinite Creativity. Infinite Abundance, pure Wisdom and perfect Wholeness exist only through and as this One, the God of my understanding.

(Unification) All of the qualities of God are already within me, for I am one of the good things It has brought forth. I am made in Its likeness and image, an individualized center in Spirit, created to reveal the Magnificence of my Creator. Everything that I am is the Glory of God made manifest, and it is Good.

(Realization) And so I rest in the realization of deepest gratitude for all of the Good that is. For the Bounty of the forest and the Peace of the sea; for the Grace of a dancer and the Beauty of fine art; for the Joy of laughing children and the surrender of praying mothers; for every bit of this and more I stand in powerful awe and appreciation. All of this Magnificence has been given to us freely to express the Power and Infinitude of the Universal Presence, and I am honored and humbled to stand witness to Its Glory.

(Thanksgiving) I give thanks upon thanks for the Truth of what is.

(Release) I release this Word of gratitude into the Law, knowing that It calls forth more to be thankful for. We are so blessed. And so it is.

# PRAYER FOR FULL EXPRESSION

(Recognition) There is One Presence, One Power, One Creator Source of All of Life, perfect, whole and complete. This One is the Love and the Law, the means of manifestation and the reason for existence. Omnipotent, everywhere present, this One is all there is. It expresses as every person, everything in the Universe. Each is perfect, Divinely created to express fully as Creativity, Beauty and Truth.

(Unification) I recognize that I am one with this One. Spirit is all there is, and I am made up of that Stuff and Substance which set the stars in motion. Every attribute of the Divine One is mine now – complete Unity with all of Life, Harmony, Love, Peace, Grace. Everywhere I go, there is God. Everything I think, there is God. Everywhere I am, there is God. I am the Divine Creativity of the entire Universe.

(Realization) Recognizing the Truth of my Divine nature, I speak my Word now for the Perfection and Grace of my full expression. I claim and affirm the Presence of Divine Intelligence in the core of my being. Always, in every moment, the Beauty and Magnificence of The One shines in, through and as me. Every situation, every seeming circumstance, all crumble before the Truth of Universal Unity and Wholeness. I impress my thoughts upon the Law, expressing all that I am, and Spirit provides all that I need for its manifestation. I am in perfect Integrity with my own Divine Beingness, sharing my full self openly with confidence. All is well, right here and right now.

(Thanksgiving) I am so thankful to stand witness to the Truth of this Word, grateful for the perfect Self-expression of all that I am, right here and right now.

(Release) With complete conviction, I release this prayer into the Law of Mind, trusting that It automatically works for the highest and best of all. I call it good. And so it is.

# PRAYER FOR BALANCE

(**Recognition**) The fullness of God is everywhere in expression, as life of all kinds. Every tree, every bird, every person is the Divine in form. It is Grace, and Love and flowing Abundance, pouring forth naturally all around. This One Spirit is sweet Balance, as the cycle of life and the reception and release of energy. The One Mind leads and directs all in perfect Balance.

(**Unification**) The Truth I know for myself is that I am one with that One Spirit, made in Its likeness and Its image. Therefore, every attribute of The One already been built into my very beingness. So, I am that Grace and Love, that Abundance and Balance, just as I am.

(**Realization**) And so, seeing myself through the lens of who I really am, I speak my word affirming that the Balance I am is activated powerfully. It shows up as productive work and joyful rest, as the natural flow and ease of activity in my life. I am guided perfectly and beautifully to Divine Right Action in every situation for the best expression of Balance in my life. I always have more than I need, and I rest and play with ease.

(**Thanksgiving**) Gratitude flows through my being, as I am overjoyed that I live in beautiful Balance right now.

(**Release**) I release this Word into the Law with absolute confidence, knowing that it is already done. And so it is.

# PRAYER FOR MY HIGHEST AND BEST

(Recognition) There is only One -- One Life, One Truth, One Presence. We call this One by many names: God, Spirit, Love, Source. And what we know about this One is that It is all there is. It created the Universe and everything in it, every person, in Its own likeness. So every person, everything, is an extension of the One Source. The very Energy that set the stars in motion is present right here and right now. It is confidence and trust and Infinite Intelligence. It is the pouring-forth of abundance and the ever-givingness of Life.

(Unification) And what I recognize is that I am an expression of this One Power. I am made up of God Stuff, and so I am all that I claim for God. I am whole, perfect and complete just as I am, and just as I am not. I am confidence and trust, Divine Intelligence and Abundance. I am Divinely guided to perfect right action and right outcome in every area of my life.

(Realization) And as I see my true nature, I speak my Word now, claiming and affirming that Life is unfolding perfectly and beautifully for me right here and right now. I am Peace, Joy and Calm in every area of my life. I am Abundance and Prosperity, with more than enough financial resources to meet my needs and plenty more to share. Spirit is my Supply and Source, and I am perfectly supplied in every single way. The entire Universe is conspiring to bring me my Good, in the form of loving relationships, prosperous living, connected spirituality and Ease in every area of my life. Any and all thoughts, beliefs or habits around fear, worry or uncertainty are just gone, back to the nothingness from which they came, for they have no power. Everything is working out for my highest and best.

(Thanksgiving) I am so thankful to stand witness to this Truth, knowing it is already manifest in my life now.

(Release) And so I release this Word into the action of Universal Law. I let it go, with confidence and gratitude, knowing it is done. And so it is.

# RESOURCES

## WAYS TO LEARN MORE

**One-on-One Spiritual Mentoring**: Relationships, career, health, abundance, life purpose -- Everything works better when you put Spirit first. We will work together to release your hidden beliefs, open up to spiritual Truth and find some relief through customized affirmative prayer. (Spiritual Mentoring sessions last between 60-90 minutes, allowing for the natural variation of insight. No additional fees will be charged for sessions that last longer than 60 minutes. Sessions can be local in Phoenix, Arizona or via teleconferencing technology worldwide.) Book a mentoring session at http://www.lezligoodwin.com

**Classes:** I am a huge fan of taking spiritual growth classes. Working in a group of like-minded individuals toward a common goal is a uniquely joyful experience. There are a number of ways you can move your spiritual education and affirmative prayer practice forward through classes.

- Take a class at your local Center for Spiritual Living. There are nearly 400 Centers worldwide, and odds are there is a Center near you. Check online, or look at the directory in the Science of Mind Magazine. (While you're at it, subscribe to Science of Mind Magazine, to take advantage of their fabulous articles and amazing Daily Guides for prayer and contemplation.)

- Take an online class through Centers for Spiritual Living. If you don't have a Center near you, there are fantastic online classes offered through CSL. These classes use teleconferencing technology so you can see and converse with your fellow students and teachers. Thank God for technology! Learn more at http://www.csl.org

- Take an online class with me! I offer Live Classes, offered via teleconferencing technology in real time. I also offer recorded classes that you can do at your own pace whenever you like. Everyone is different and life is complex – only you know what works for you, so I give you lots of options. Learn more and register at http://www.lezligoodwin.com/onlineclasses

**Join our Facebook Group:** Connect with people all over the world who are working on the same things you are by joining our *Wisdom Everyday* Facebook Group. Share your successes, get inspired, learn more about affirmative prayer and begin living the life of your dreams. Join at: https://www.facebook.com/groups/wisdomwednesday/

**Subscribe to our Sexy Spirituality Podcast:** Every week, we discuss real spiritual topics that are relevant to modern life. Messy, funny, authentic, joyful, real people talking about a spirituality that isn't a separate topic, but is a part of every area of life. The best part is that it's free! Listen at http://sexyspiritualitypodcast.com

**Subscribe to my YouTube Channel:** Do you ever need a spiritual pick-me-up at 2:00 AM on a Tuesday? Or 4:45 PM on a Saturday? The awesome thing about YouTube videos is that you can access them at any time, day or night. I post Sunday Service messages, affirmative prayers, informational sessions and more. You can access all of this good stuff at https://tinyurl.com/y9d2672q

**Read my Blog:** As someone who has dedicated my whole life to learning, living and teaching spirituality, I have some things to say on the topic. My favorite way to share my day-to-day insights are on my blog. I genuinely believe that everything in life is spiritual, so every topic is open for conversation. It's free, of course, and easy to access at https://www.lezligoodwin.com/blog

## Additional Resources

Science of Mind Magazine is a monthly periodical that includes daily spiritual guides, articles on New Thought ideas and wonderful features to fuel your expansive life. Learn more and subscribe at https://scienceofmind.com/

*This Thing Called You*, by Ernest Holmes. This is my absolute favorite book from Dr. Holmes, the founder of Science of Mind. It's an easy read, sweet and heart-opening. It's my go-to choice when I need comforting. Learn more at https://g.co/kgs/Dy98qh

*You are a Badass: How to Stop Doubting Your Greatness and Start Living and Awesome Life*, by Jen Sincero. This book is amazing for people who are new to New Thought and just need some straight talk about manifesting, getting past limiting beliefs and being your best self. Learn more at https://g.co/kgs/F6W6Qn

# TEMPLATE FOR 5-STEP AFFIRMATIVE PRAYER

## PREP STEPS

Problem:

Quality:

Purpose:

## 5 STEPS OF AFFIRMATIVE PRAYER

Recognition:




Unification:

Realization:




Thanksgiving:




Release:

# LIST OF SPIRITUAL QUALITIES

| | |
|---|---|
| Abundance | Love |
| Balance | Oneness |
| Beauty | Order |
| Ease | Peace |
| Freedom | Power |
| Good | Prosperity |
| Grace | Truth |
| Intelligence | Unity |
| Joy | Wholeness |
| Light | Wisdom |

# LIST OF NAMES FOR GOD

| | |
|---|---|
| All-That-Is | Infinite Presence |
| The All-Good | Love |
| Almighty Divine | Light |
| The Beloved | The One |
| Creator | The One Mind |
| Creator Source | Power |
| Divine Creator | Presence |
| Divine Mind | The Source |
| Divine Wisdom | Source Energy |
| Energy | Spirit |
| God | Sweet Spirit |
| God-the-Good | Truth |
| Good/Goodness | The Universe |
| The Infinite | Wisdom |

Made in the USA
Las Vegas, NV
29 November 2021